ARE YE DANCIN'?

BURNTISLAND PALAIS DE DANSE

ROBERT HUTTON, Proprietor and Manager

"Where youth and pleasure meet
To chase the glowing hours with flying feet."

WEDNESDAY - POPULAR NIGHT
8 to 11. Ladies 9d.: Gents 1/-.

SATURDAY - CARNIVAL NIGHT
8 to 11. Ladies 1/-: Gents 1/6.

SPECIAL DANCES
arranged during Holidays

THE MOST POPULAR
WITH THE PERFECT

MANSE L

ISLA

EXTRACT FROM RULES

No intoxicating liquor will be brought into or consumed in the Club.

Members only allowed one guest per evening.

The management reserves the right to refuse admission.

Membership card must be produced on request.

Members will be responsible for their guests.

NAME

ADDRES

DATE

SIGNATU

N

CLUB PICASSO
200 BUCHANAN STREET
GLASGOW, C.1

MEMBERSHIP CARD

nicked at FLICKS

Nº 1 SIZE
SLIPPERINE
REGISTERED
DANCE POLISH
AN IMMEDIATE & LASTING
POLISH WITHOUT LABOUR

"SLIPPERINE" TRADE MARK IS REGISTERED IN THE
ISLES THE IRISH FREE STATE, CANADA &

ARE YE DANCIN'?

The story of Scotland's dance halls, rock'n'roll, and how yer da met yer maw

Eddie Tobin

with Martin Kielty

WAVERLEY BOOKS

THE PYTHONS
SKIFFLE GROUP

PAVILION
BALLROOM
RESTAURANT

er and Better Every Week!

NTY F.C. AMENITIES COMMITTEE

rday Night
ANCES

Acknowledgments

Eddie and Martin would like to thank all those
who have given their time, pictures and quotes for the book.

First published 2010 by Waverley Books, 144 Port Dundas Road,
Glasgow, G4 0HZ, Scotland, UK.

© 2010 Eddie Tobin and Martin Kielty.

A catalogue entry for this book is available from the British Library.

ISBN: 978-1-84934-045-8

Set in 10.5 on 13.3pt Georgia and Helvetica Neue.

Designed and produced by Martin Kielty.

Printed and bound in the EU.

Picture credits:

Cover & Pviii main pic from Sensational Alex Harvey Band's collection; Pii
(Slipperine) Brytaflor & Dunston Furnishings Ltd, (Dansette) Ewan Gordon; Piv-v Edo
Brown/Derek Brown, (Pythons) Roy Kitley, (The 'Strathy') Arthur Scott, (Apollo) Anne
Fitzsimmons; Pviii-ix [trumpeter, bass and box players] Bert MacKay, [Mike Sata &
the Hellcats] Arthur Scott, [Teddy boys] Stewart Campbell, [Pathfinders] "242
Showbeat Magazine"; Pxi Anwar Hussein/Getty Images. Pxii Max Langdon; P3 Ian
Dickson/Mountain; P4, 6-7 Scottish Screen Archive; P9 Courtesy of NEFA,
Aberdeenshire Council; P10 Portnellan Highland Lodges www.portnellan.com; P13
Burntisland Heritage Trust; P14 (jukebox) Lara Goetsch, Timeline Theatre Company,
Chicago, Illinois, USA; (Dansette) Ewan Gordon; P16 (Archie Semple) Malcom Burns
with thanks to Ian Maund; (Cherry Grant) Brian Nobile archive; P21 Missouri Valley
Special Collections, Kansas City Public Library; P22-27, 178-79 Edo Brown/Derek
Brown; P28 Shutterstock/Alex Kosev; P31 Roy Kitley; P32 Universal/Decca; P35
Stewart Campbell; P37 IPC Publications; P42 Peter Kerr; P48 (Lulu), 71, 101, 105 (Jim
Sinclair), 108–9, 129, (Clan Ball) 178, 179 "242 Showbeat Magazine"; P52 Courtesy of
the Columbia Tristar Motion Picture Group by arrangement with Sony Pictures; P55,
88, 140, 171 Arthur Scott archive; P56–57 Bert MacKay; P58–59, 74, 179 Brian Nobile
archive; P61 James Grimes; P68 (main pic) Stewart Campbell; (OMO) Courtesy of
Unilever; P70 Pat McCann; P78–79 Martin Griffiths; P85 Frank Ferri; P95-96, 132-133
Ronnie Anderson; P106, 117, 118-119 "Moody" magazine; P110 Beatstalkers' own
collection; P111, 179 Alan Mair; P113 Daily Record; P124 in2ballroom; P128, 145
Courtesy of Brian Beacom; P132 (Apollo) Anne Fitzsimmons; P134-35 "Rock
Superstars" magazine; P140 Arthur Scott archive; P141 Jim Summaria; P144 Gordon
Nicol; P149 Courtesy of Paramount Pictures; P152 Cheeky Easdale; P154, 170 BBC;
P160 Gordon Gurvan archive; P162 Sony.

While Martin Kielty has made great effort to trace and credit all copyright holders he
would be glad to hear from any who may have been omitted.

CONTENTS

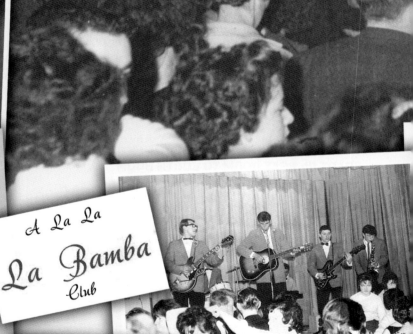

The PATHFINDERS

Foreword

I cut my teeth as a musician in the halls of Scotland – and I can tell you it was some education. I have so many memories of travelling the highways and byways starting in the early 1970s, going to play all sorts of gigs Eddie had booked for my bands. I could fill this book myself. But it's time for other people to have their say so I'll just rhyme off a few of my favourite – and least favourite – places to play.

The scariest hall I ever went to was the Kirkintilloch Town Hall. I think it was called the Graveyard because all the bad guys used to go there to batter everyone on a Saturday. Nope, I don't ever want to go back to the Kirkintilloch Town Hall.

All the best-looking women were in the Electric Garden in Glasgow. It was the time when all the women wore very short skirts. I was about seventeen or eighteen in that era – what can I say? My hormones were running wild, the women were running wild, and I was a happy man in the Electric Garden.

The JM Ballroom in Dundee was another very good-looking crowd. The girls weren't quite as good-looking as in Glasgow, to my eye anyway, but they were certainly much more generous to members of whatever bands happened by.

The best place to play in Scotland for me was Clouds in Glasgow. We always had hundreds of fans shouting for us and supporting everything we did there. And it meant we could say we played the Apollo – okay, it wasn't actually the Apollo but it was upstairs from that legendary hall, which was close enough for our purposes. Later on, my band Salvation did play the Apollo with Tiger Tim, and of course I came back when I was in Ultravox.

Another fabulous gig was the Burns Howff in Glasgow's West Regent Street. It was a pub rather than a dance hall but it contributed a lot to the quality of the bands people danced to in bigger places. We only got paid ten pounds but all the best bands played there. You had to have done the Howff – if you hadn't you were a plonker. So we tried and tried – and finally got to play there. Plonkerness avoided!

Midge performing with his band Slick in 1975   Photo: Anwar Hussein/Getty Images

A long-haired Midge and his band Salvation play Clouds in Glasgow, 'the best place to play in Scotland'   Photo: Max Langdon

One final memorable place, for slightly different reasons: Cumnock Town Hall in Ayrshire. Every Friday you had to fight your way in and fight your way back out. The fighting revolved around the fact that people from nearby Auchinleck didn't like people from Cumnock. All the guys in the room ended up covered in blood. But it had a positive side – if we could keep the music going we could escape relatively unscathed, so we learned the art of continuing to play no matter what.

Some of these places have gone and some are still part of Scotland's nightlife – but they all have more great stories to tell and I think you'll enjoy a lot of the ones in Eddie's book. I did!

MIDGE URE, August 2010

Montage spreads:
Page ii: Burntisland Palais de Danse flier; Club Picasso's membership card; a coaster from Flicks nightclub; a Dansette record player; Slipperine dance-floor polish.
Pages iv-v: Main pic: JM Ballroon Dundee. Left to right: Dave Marshall and Bill Morrison of the Grove Nicol Orchestra; the Pythons Skiffle group; the "Strathy", the Pavilion Ballroom Strathpeffer; Glasgow's much-missed Apollo Theatre.
Pages viii-ix: Main pic: the Alex Harvey Soul Band. From top left: Tiger Tim's first business card; Melotones trumpeter Fergie Brown; Cavendish press ad; La Bamba and Hollywood Boulevard promo cards; Mike Sata and the Hell Cats; more Melotones in action; Stuart Campbell's Edinburgh gang of "Deaf Teds"; the Pathfinders.
Pages 178-79: Main pic: Edo Brown playing with the Johnny Kennoway Band. Left to right: Edo Brown playing bass, the Red Hawks; (pirate) Radio Scotland's Clan Ball in Dundee; the Beatstalkers; Radio Scotland's short-lived publication, 242 Showbeat Magazine.

ARE YE DANCIN'?

Introduction: 'I was astute enough to fire the drummer since he only had a wheel'

IN 1965, when I was 17, I retired. I'd been working as an apprentice shipping clerk for a refrigeration company. But in the era where the Beatles and the Stones were at their height, and we were young men, the Bo Weavles' band meetings were clearly generating hits. So I decided to retire and manage the band. I was astute enough to fire the drummer right away, because he didn't have a drum kit – he just had a wheel with sticks stuck in it to make a noise.

We didn't make loads of money at first but we had a lot of fun and met a lot of wonderful people, including some very wonderful girls. The band grew until I was 22, and by then they had a reputation. We weren't the top band in Scotland – but we were definitely top five.

One of the agencies that used the band was Ronnie Simpson's Music and Cabaret. Everyone who ran a successful band worked in an agency so Ronnie asked me, 'Why don't you work here?' Then when someone phoned to book the Bo Weavles I could say, 'We're not available, but this other act is ...' And that's how Ronnie grew the agency.

The heavy rock revolution arrived and the Bo Weavles became Tear Gas. One day I was in the office with Derek Nicol, an agent who'd started in the east coast, and a wee fat man came in with a Revox tape recorder. His name was Bill Fehilly and he'd made a lot of money out of bingo halls. He had a tape of a singer from Birmingham, who he thought was the new Tom Jones, and wanted to know what we thought – should he manage the guy?

I listened to the tape and it was rubbish. Derek was more astute than I was – he was from Fife, Nazareth were from Fife, he represented Nazareth and they'd just made a great tape. So he said to Bill: 'I'll play you a tape ...' Bill was blown away, 'Tom Jones' went on the back burner and he said, as all millionaires say, 'Why don't we open an office in London? We'll all be rich and famous ...' So Derek went to London to work with Bill and Nazareth.

A while later, Derek and Bill took me to down south to see Alex Harvey. I knew him from his Soul Band days but I thought he was yesterday's man. Still, I went to see him: he was really offensive, really aggressive, and he was doing everything he'd become famous for. He was incredibly intense – scary. You were thinking: 'I hope he doesn't come off the stage and get *me*.'

Derek asked if I could find a band to put Alex in with. I suggested Tear Gas, who were doing

My charges: the Sensational Alex Harvey Band at the height of their success

well but were running out of ways to do better. The story's a legend in itself – one afternoon in 1972 Alex met the band in Glasgow, they went into a rehearsal room, jammed 'Midnight Moses' and were immediately sensational. They were made for each other and the word 'sensational' was accurate – and that was the Sensational Alex Harvey Band.

So I went to London and worked for Bill's Mountain Management. I was also doing my other things, plugging records, buying records into the charts and all that. Everyone was happy for a few years.

One night I went to a late-night Nazareth show and some heavy-duty music journalists were there. It wasn't a perfect set but I think they did well. But Bill came into the dressing room and started tearing strips off the band in front of all these industry guys.

Bill was a very angry man, a very scary man, but he was out of order. I still have no idea what it was all about, but I took the band out of the venue to get them away from it, then went back to the office at eight in the morning, where Bill was still insisting he'd been right. I said: 'That was a disgrace – you've embarrassed me, the band, the company ...' and Bill started smashing things up in the office, which was a very expensive place. The Beatles manager,

Allen Klein, was next door and the decor was by Harrods, so he was smashing some valuable things as he insisted he was right. He told me: 'If I say black is white, it's white.' I said: 'Not to me it's not,' got the secretary to book me a flight to Scotland, and went home.

When I got back to Glasgow I went into the Clouds nightclub to see the owner, Frank Lynch. I wasn't looking for work – I just went to see him for a laugh because I liked him. But he asked me what I was doing and when I admitted I had no idea, Frank said: 'I'll give you an office, a salary and a secretary – work for me, do whatever you do, I don't care.' Which was a great opportunity, so I didn't say no.

So I sat down in my new office and thought: 'What do I do? Well, I'm a manager and I'm an agent, so why don't I do that?' My idea was to get the best rock act, the best folk act, the best cabaret act, and run them. That way, everyone would phone my office because I had the best acts, and that's how I'd grow the business and become famous.

So I signed Chris McClure, I built Salvation around Midge Ure, I signed Billy Connolly and soon I was managing loads of bands, radio DJs, TV presenters and so on. It took off so well that Frank gave me a car one day. I'd never been given a car and I didn't know how to deal with it – so I just ignored it ... Frank was waiting in his office for me to rush in and say thanks, but I just pretended it hadn't happened. Three days later he came into my office and said: 'Did you actually *get* the car?' It

Legend: The Glasgow Apollo, opened in 1973

must have seemed extremely ungrateful. It was a terrible thing to do, but I didn't mean it ...

Billy Connolly was a folk act at the time but I couldn't grow his career in the folk clubs. So I found a way to get him out of those clubs and onto bigger shows. I got 10,000 posters made and paid someone to post them all over Glasgow, which hadn't been done before. We sold out the Pavilion Theatre almost instantly, took him on two sold-out tours and the rest is history.

By this time we'd blown Ronnie Simpson's agency away, so I got him in to work for me. I don't think Ronnie ever got the credit for what he did in Scotland – the caveman who invented the wheel isn't the caveman who got the credit for doing it. Ronnie invented the wheel for the music business in Scotland.

Our next trick was to come up with the name for the Glasgow Apollo, which was what we called Green's Playhouse when we took it over. Clouds was doing so well we could afford to run the whole building, and of course that place is a legend all by itself. We named it after an album Ronnie owned, James Brown Live at the Apollo. Frank Lynch tells everyone it's because it was a short word and the signage would be cheap, but that's just because he thinks it's a better story.

We gave it the name because we wanted to be associated with the Apollo in Harlem. We even used the same lettering. If you could do that and make it work, we'd all be famous. And it *did* work. Ronnie even came up with the idea of giving people a statue, the Apollo Oscar, if they sold the place out. People all over the world still have them, except Johnny Cash who binned his the night we gave it to him.

I always think things will last for ever, but it's not always true. Frank and I found ourselves in a dispute over Billy's contract, and we fell out. So I moved on – I went to work with Colin Robertson, who'd been a manager in the early days of the Apollo but had moved on. He was running the Shuffles club in Glasgow and I went over there, while still managing artists, DJs and so on.

By the mid 1980s I had the deals to represent both the Old Firm's first teams. It transpired that none of those players had representation but needed it, so I approached both companies and offered my services, and wound up with all the contracts. Around the same time, Colin decided to move on from Shuffles, so I took it over as the Mayfair, and that was the first time I was responsible for the staff, the crowd, the light bulbs – the whole thing. With the generosity of Ross Bowie, the building's owner, I did very well after a shaky start.

It was all going well and I was approached to become an area manager for Stakis, who owned a lot of clubs. But the company monitored all its incoming calls and I was receiving more calls about artists, and about Ally McCoist, than about official Stakis business. So they asked me to make a decision, and I decided to become a real area manager.

The company was sold to Scottish and Newcastle who gave me even more pubs and clubs to run. They offered me a directorship of the company, and my region would be Rotherham to Aberdeen. I wouldn't go to Rotherham to visit the lavatory – it's the end of the earth. Hotel California is in Rotherham. So when Carnegie Leisure offered me a directorship I took that instead.

Around ten years ago I decided to stop working at Carnegie's and learn how to play golf, and I spent four months catching up, and saying thank you to with people who'd helped me. I don't think people ever thank other people enough, so it's nice to be able to take the time to go back.

I was then offered a directorship with Upfront Security – not a working role, just an associate role to advise in a licensing capacity, which they thought might help. In a matter of weeks I was the managing director and I enjoyed five successful and happy years there.

I decided to leave that to do my own thing. I formed Cleaning Scotland, Security Scotland, Training Scotland and Entertainment Scotland, and I thought: 'Surely I've got to enjoy one of them!' Those plates are spinning, and where they stop nobody knows.

It's great to have received a lifetime achievement award from the licensed trade industry. But I can't help wondering if there's enough time to earn another one – can you, in one lifetime, do enough to merit two? *That's* the challenge!

Meanwhile I have time to look back at some of the great laughs I've had over the years in all these wonderful dance halls, working with some great people, and entertaining the best audience in the world: the people of Scotland. This book only scratches the surface, but it proves we all feel the same way about the dancin' and what it's about: passion, great music, and meeting great people.

EDDIE TOBIN, July 2010

1100s~1950s

Dancing started out as a war weapon – but in association with new music of the 20th century became the mascot of peace and love. Most of the time ...

REBELS WITH THE RIGHT MOVES

1 I actually used the line 'Do you come here often?'

WHAT do William Wallace, Robert the Bruce, Angus Og, Bonnie Prince Charlie, Sir Walter Scott, Sir Harry Lauder and Sean Connery all have in common – asides from being Scottish?

They all met their wives by saying: 'Are ye dancin'?'

They're not alone. That's the way many millions and probably billions of relationships have started in Scotland since the dancin' began in the twelfth century.

It's all changed now, of course – and it was always changing. But two things stayed at the heart of the dancin' for over 900 years. One, you wanted to meet a member of the opposite sex. Two, he actually did say: *'Are ye dancin'?'* She actually did say: *'Are ye askin'?'* He actually did say: *'Ah'm askin''*. And she actually did say: *'Ah'm dancin''*. If he was lucky. If he wasn't, she might say, *'Naw, it's just the way I'm standin'*, *'Naw, the doctor sent me here to convalesce'*, or much much worse.

The origins of the dancin' can be traced back to the 1100s, when Scotland was just getting the hang of being a nation. Legend says Highland dance is one of the oldest forms of folk dance in the world, and forms like ballet and square dancing came out of it.

But it didn't quite start out as a way for a guy to meet his girl. It really started as a way for the king to choose the fittest men for battle – if you could do a reel, a sword-dance and a jig then toss a caber and swim a loch, you were worth having up the front when the English came to call. The military training aspect of Highland dance survived until quite recently among Scottish regiments.

Of course, that's the 'official' history – everyone had been dancing at ceilidhs since the beginning of time and no one ever felt any need to stop. But the more ornate style of performance came seriously into fashion in the Victorian era, when the queen and her nobles liked nothing more than to spend a few weeks in their northern lands; this was before Spain became a popular holiday destination, obviously. By that time it was not only a finely-honed art – it was an art almost exclusively performed by men.

By the early 1900s the ladies got in on the act and over the following century it became common for larger towns and cities to have some kind of ballroom – although they weren't

For those and such as those: ballroom dancing in the early 1800s before being popularised in the Victorian era

often open to the public. Edinburgh's Assembly Rooms began hosting public dances in the 1870s, then in 1905 the first purpose-built public venue, Glasgow's Albert Hall, opened its doors. Within 25 years most people did one of two things with their spare time: they went to the pictures or they went to the dancin'. Probably in the other order, of course, when you think about it, especially if you were trying to meet prospective partners.

Another technological advance spurred the dancin' on: the charabanc. The forerunner to the modern bus hadn't often been seen on Scotland's dubious Highland roads while it was horse-drawn machinery, but when it acquired an engine in the early 1920s it soon became an important method of transport. The rail network was wider-ranging then than it is now but a charabanc could take you door-to-door from one village hall to another.

So the concert parties began to travel – groups of 12 to 20 people learned a few folk songs, wrote a few poems, rehearsed a few dances then jumped into a charabanc to travel a few dozen miles to a village they'd never seen before. A few weeks later their new friends returned the favour, so all over the place you had touring artists adding outside interest to the village hall ceilidhs. The word 'ceilidh' means 'visit', incidentally, and with more than 400 halls springing to life with new arrivals, never had the word been more appropriate.

SHONA WALLACE: You laugh now, but leaving Fort William was quite a big thing for me when I was a 19-year-old girl – even if we were only going the ten miles to Ballachulish.

There were about fifteen of us in our concert party and at least once every six weeks it was our turn to go out and perform somewhere else. I learned a new poem every time that I'd sing, maybe with a bit of fiddle for accompaniment, and everyone else did their bit too. You had dancers, storytellers, musicians – we really tried to make a good night of it and you always wanted to do better than the other village would when it was their turn to visit you.

I had a dance or two with the young men in the other halls but there was always someone from home keeping an eye on me. Girls just didn't drink in those days or people would say awful things about you – especially if you were found actually drunk. You didn't see all that many men drunk either. Most of them took a drink but they could always look after themselves, but there were one or two who you'd see being pointed the road home sometimes, especially if they were just home from the merchant navy and could afford an extra bit of whisky.

The charabanc bus was often a cold thing to be in. There was a canvas roof which came over if it rained, but it didn't keep any heat in. So sometimes you'd be frozen to the bone by the time you got to the dance, and you were certainly frozen to the bone on the way home again. One night it toppled over on the road out to Spean Bridge. One fellow broke his ankle but that was all – I heard a lot worse could happen. They weren't very good at staying upright.

Necessary evil: early charabancs were exposed and top-heavy

LORNA CHRISTIE: In Aberdeenshire, village dances were usually compered by the minister or a shopkeeper or another local worthy. My friend Anne was a beautiful wee thing – all the lads were after her. So when the compere said, 'Take your parters,' and went to put the record on the Dansette record player, all the lads would charge at her – and fall over each other in a big heap on the floor. You'd think we'd have been jealous of Anne but she always got embarrassed about it and we all thought it was funny. When a loon finally came up to you and said, 'Are ye dancin'?' I'd say, 'Were ye no' at the top of the heap then?'

Dances were always on Friday nights. They started at 10pm and went on until midnight, when they stopped for tea and sandwiches. Then they went on till 2am. We used to cycle for miles except when a friend of mine who didn't have a bike was going, then we just walked. If you were working on the Saturday morning you didn't think twice about getting up and getting on with it.

Out in the wilderness – that is, *really* out there, since most of Scotland was a wilderness until quite recently – farming communities had their own type of party, known as a kirn.

Everyone would decorate the biggest barn and the travelling fiddlers would arrive and join those locals who could play, then it was dancing, partying and drinking till the wee hours.

As the big-band era wound to a climax in the big cities, some of those musicians managed to make their way into the wilderness and meet new fans. Inspired by the experience, those who could afford it bought their own instruments and started playing along to their 78 rpm shellac records. Thing were looking up – until World War II began in 1939.

On the commencement of hostilities on September 3, all public dance halls were closed. It didn't seem right to be having fun while there was a war on. A few weeks later, though, the powers-that-be realised there wasn't actually anything else to do except have fun while there was a war on – and the dancin' began again.

Some halls, including the Oddfellows Hall in North Berwick, became known as 'The Sweatbox', because once the blackout curtains were in place there was no way for the heat and smoke to escape the room. Others didn't get the opportunity to reopen, and instead were taken over by the army for use as training areas or billets. These included the Burma Ballroom in Kirkcaldy, the Marine Ballroom in Arbroath and the Kinema Ballroom in Dunfermline – even though the Kinema had only been open a year. Stories abound of venue managers, who often lived in flats attached to the premises, going to extreme measures like laying lino in order to protect their precious sprung dancefloors from British and Polish troops' feet.

Of course, the war brought another novelty to Scotland: the Yanks. It was a culture-shock for everyday Scots to meet these gum-chewing American guys from across the Atlantic ... and it was a very different kind of culture-shock for the men than it was for the women. When the war ended, many new relationships didn't – the Americans were oversexed, overpaid and over here, and weren't about to go home.

Fortunately Scotland is an island nation full of ports, and people are mainly used to living with people who don't agree with their way of life. So there was a lot to celebrate when the war ended and everyone realised there was a new musical direction to explore.

Jazz was the music of the era and like so many forms of music it had started off as the 'noise' your parents hated. By the post-war era it was completely mainstream and considered the 'pop' of its day.

FRANK FERRI: I was aged 14 and there was nothing to do of a Sunday night in Edinburgh in those days. Everything – shops, cinemas, everything – was closed. All we could do was wander the streets, which is what my mate Billy Harper and I were doing when we passed a small doorway at the side of Woolworth's in Leith. We heard music coming from the Palace Ballroom on the third floor above Woolies.

Curiosity aroused, we climbed the stairs until a man appeared above us. We had great respect for adults in those days, so we were ready to run, but we stuttered, 'Can we get in?'

BURNTISLAND
PALAIS DE DANSE

ROBERT HUTTON, Proprietor and Manager

"Where youth and pleasure meet
To chase the glowing hours with flying feet."

WEDNESDAY - POPULAR NIGHT
8 to 11. Ladies 9d.: Gents 1/-.

SATURDAY - CARNIVAL NIGHT
8 to 11. Ladies 1/-: Gents 1/6.

> SPECIAL DANCES
> arranged during Holidays

THE MOST POPULAR PALAIS
WITH THE PERFECT FLOOR

MANSE LANE
BURNTISLAND

Into the war and out again: the Burntisland Palais survived the ravages of global conflict with its house band, right, continuing to offer pleasure in the glowing hours as it had in previous years, above

MINISTRY OF
FOOD
953-1954

RATION BOOK

SERIAL NO.
VB 313151

MF

Surname:

Address:

IF FOUND
RETURN TO
ANY FOOD
OFFICE

F.O. CODE No.
L — O
6

**Spirit of Britain:
wartime poster,
right, post-war
ration book,
top, 1950s
jukebox,
above, and
Dansette
record player,
below**

KEEP
CALM
AND
CARRY
ON

'Yes,' he replied, 'If you've got one and ninepence,' which is about eight and a half pence in today's money. Fortunately we did have it, so we went in. The old dance hall had a stage, with the floor interrupted by pillars. We took our place at a table and became aware of a huge wall of sound exploding from the band on stage. On reflection it wasn't loud by today's standards – for a start it wasn't amplified. But we'd never heard live music in an enclosed space before.

It was Archie Semple on stage and that night he inspired a life-long interest in Dixieland jazz for me. We sat through the whole performance and our one and ninepence even got us a cup of tea and two cakes. Billy and I felt quite grown-up in this strange new environment.

SANDRA CAIRNS: The Palace was run by Professor Wood and for a short time the house band included Beatrice Mackenzie on piano, playing wartime songs like Roll Out the Barrel. My mother was happy to let me go to the Palace because it was run by a professor and had a woman in the band – and she lived in our street too. Professor Wood invented some famous waltzes of the day: the Pride of Erin, the Waverley and the Windsor. He won an international dancing competition when he was in his 70s and retired at the grand old age of 80. I'm not the only one who owes him a debt of gratitude for a lifetime of dancing.

BRIAN HALE: I was an artificer apprentice at HMS Caledonia at Rosyth in 1948, along with about 700 others. Visits to the Kinema in Dunfermline – we called it the Kin – were the highlight of a run ashore. I remember those evenings more clearly than I remember what I did yesterday: the smell of the ballroom, perfume, hair cream and smoke; the mirrorball in the ceiling; and Cherry, the hostess who kept us all in order.

Like a lot of the lads I met a lot of girlfriends there, and if I was lucky had the chance to take them through the back door to, em, cool off. Then it was back to the dancing with quicksteps, foxtrots and waltzes. There was a favourite in the Kin called 'Kiss Me Once, Kiss Me More' – I think it was written in the area.

Our leave expired at 10.30 so we always had to make an early exit, much to the relief of the local lads, I'd say. Then it was a mad dash to the bus station and back to the docks.

PETER McCABE: We had the Palais in Burntisland but it was a bit dull, full of older folk who were more interested in dancing to the same tunes every night than hearing something new. So we used to go the Kin – and you had to get there early because it always filled up quickly. The band would play new stuff all the time, but you had to be careful not to get caught out with a dance you didn't know. If that happened you tried to get near Cherry and follow what she was doing. She saved many a young man's blushes!

The Kinema's Cherry Grant was a well-known local character, although many halls had people who filled the same role. She taught dancing in between roles as a professional entertainer, but she's most remembered for her role as hostess – almost like a mistress of ceremonies and steward rolled into one. If you misbehaved you had to answer to her ... although most people didn't dare, preferring to enjoy her life-and-soul-of-the-party face rather than her angry-schoolteacher act.

Dance teachers were very common on the ground, because the dancin' had a set of rules you had to learn. The days of lumbering from one foot to the other were many decades in the future. While there were travelling tutors in the Highlands, setting up shop in schools, barns and shed, in the bigger towns and cities you went to classes run at the places you'd later be dancing in.

Archie Semple

ANDY DUFF: I first went to Stewart's School of Dancing in Edinburgh in 1954. It was divided into three parts with beginners going to the Edina in Surgeon's Hall. My first night ended in disaster – I was kicked out for making a fool out of the instructor. She had us in a circle prancing about like fairies and I just cracked up. My mate stayed on and next day he said I was allowed to come back if I apologised and behaved in future. Talk about humble!

FRANK FERRI: I'd go to Stewart's every Saturday morning feeling quite grown up. The hall was a long rectangular shape and boys would sit to one side with the girls on the other. Mr Stewart, the owner, and his wife would start up the music and give a demonstration of the steps.

Then the music started again and those who could dance in a fashion got up and did their thing. That left the male and female wallflowers standing and just watching, until Stewart and his wife would go around the hall matching up wallflowers. Whether you could dance or not you were forced to get up – and after a few weeks of standing on toes and more embarrassing moments you became more confident.

Cherry Grant

You even started trying out immature chat-up lines, like the old standard: 'Do you come here often?' I still cringe that I actually said that – but I came to love dancing and looked forward to those Saturday mornings.

ANDY DUFF: At Stewart's in Drummond Street, you could go on to enter competitions or just enjoy the dancing and chatting up the girls. After a few weeks there you were expected to go on to the Afton, which was for advanced dancers. What really bugged me was you were looked upon as a beginner there – but this was the Friday and Saturday nights which wasn't for competitions. It was supposed to be dancing for enjoyment – to get a bird. So after a couple of weeks of that I went back to Stewart's. It had a better class of talent anyway.

Some people very quickly became fascinated with the dancin' world and it became the centre of their social life. For others it was even more important – for example, Miss Lilias Sutherland and Mr James Hood, who were married in the ballroom of the Glasgow Locarno in 1949 in exactly the place they'd met and had their first dance.

COLIN CAMPBELL: My big night ... here I was going up to the Marine, the pride of Arbroath. Me and the lads had been planning it for weeks because the Tommy Sampson Orchestra were playing and we'd heard them on the radio – plus my dad had served with Tommy in Italy during the war. I was tall for my age and I'd managed to grow a bit of a moustache by carefully keeping out of the teachers' way at school – probably the quietest month of the school's history while I was there!

In the end all the lads bottled out except me so I thought, in for a penny and all that, so I paid my two and five to get in. And there I was! Girls everywhere! I didn't waste any time – I marched up to a nice-looking blonde girl who was sitting with her friends and said, 'Can I have this dance?' She looked me up and down and replied: 'Is that meant to be a moustache or has your eyebrow come down for a break?' I stayed in the shadows for the rest of the night, but Tommy Sampson was brilliant.

2 You could actually tell the time by the tune the band were playing

AS SCOTLAND arrived in the 1950s its population broke five million for the first time and the music charts began to be counted by record sales instead of sheet music sales. Colour TV arrived, costing over $1000 a set in the USA.

There was something approaching a Scottish music circuit with, for example's sake, the Mick Mulligan Jazz Band able to tour the Drill Hall, Dumfries; Corn Exchange, Kelso; Railway Hall, Inverurie; Dalrymple Hall, Fraserburgh; St Congan's Hall, Turriff; Town Hall, Huntly and the Boys' Brigade Hall, Wick.

WILLIE BELL: I'd heard some stories about Mick Mulligan, and Roger Melly who sang for him, but that night I saw it for myself. I took my girlfriend to the Drill Hall to see them and they were truly incredible – the word 'raver' was invented for Mulligan and it wasn't wrong. Not only could he play amazingly well, playing some 1920s and 1930s stuff note-for-note on his trumpet, but he threw himself about on stage, and I think he and Melly spent a lot of the time trying to put each other off. It only made them worse.

Problem was, he was even more of a raver off stage than he was on. I could see he had his eye on my girlfriend and during the interval he came out with a bottle of whisky and tried to butt into our conversation.

I said something like, 'Oi, do you mind, leave us alone,' and Mick turned to her and said, 'Is that what you want?' She looked at me and nodded. Mick shrugged and said, 'Ah well, you were only going to be the interval entertainment anyway.'

Of course, she got upset and ran off, and in that women's way it was all my fault so she wouldn't listen to me and went home. I gave up following her and went back into the hall, and Mick was still there, so I decided to have a word with him.

He saw me coming and held out the whisky bottle, and said: 'Here – you can either hit me with it or drink it with me.' After a moment's thought I took a drink. I don't remember much of the rest of the night except Mick had heard tell of a haunted cottage in Auldgirth, where I lived, and wanted to spend the night there so he could see a ghost.

Did my girlfriend forgive me? I don't know, but we got married two years later.

Change was in the air but on the whole it was business as usual – with an edge. A press campaign started asking what was wrong with the children of Britain, saying: *'We don't seem to either have the time or patience to bring up a family. Not like our mothers had anyway, and they had a bigger job than we. I would give the "Bobby" on our beat a freer hand to administer a wallop where it hurts most. I remember the "Bobby" on our beat. The very mention of his name was enough to send me into hiding. Let's have action now, before we really get scared of them.'* Yes, back in 1952 they were saying that.

The following year saw the coronation of Queen Elizabeth II and another outraged newspaper reporter exclaiming: *'I went to a Dundee Cinema on Saturday to see* The Quiet Man, *which I thoroughly enjoyed, but at the finish of the programme, I was surprised to hear a number of Irish tunes being played instead of the National Anthem. Did the Manager genuinely forget to honour or Queen, and in Coronation Year too? I asked the Manager why – "When we played the National Anthem few people stood still," he said. "It came to be there was a rush for the exits just before the film ended. Then there were patrons who objected to those who kept on the move during the Anthem, and that caused trouble. So in the end we found it better to drop it".'*

Meanwhile, in Dundee, Miss Esther Clarke offered juvenile classes in national, tap and speciality dances, with one wag noting that tap dancing 'must be hell' for ex-servicemen who'd learned Morse code during the war. In the same city you'd pay two shillings to dance from 8pm until 11pm in the Empress Ballroom or the Dance Palais – but only one and six to see Bill Thomson and his band at the West End Palais. Edinburgh was serving the generations in a similar way for a similar price plan.

TOM WATSON: Thursday night was the night for me because it was only one and six to get into the Palais. But they had a talent show that night too and you could win free entry the next week. It wasn't all that great a prize but it was the same people entering every week. I had a bit of a voice on me so I won often enough that I was probably paying to get in three times out of every five. You could do a lot with those three extra bob! For a start you could send your niece to the children's dancing at the Palais on a Saturday morning, because that was two and six, but it included lunch. My sister-in-law was so pleased with me sending wee Lucy that she gave me dinner and sorted my clothes out for the Saturday night, which set me up fine for a night at the dancin'.

There were 11 public halls operating in Glasgow with an increasing number of bands forming to serve the market. If you were any good you could expect to earn, over two shows, what your parents earned in a week – more if you were a member of the Musicians' Union. And if you were extra lucky you could be paid for not playing at all.

GEORGE McKENZIE: I knew a lot of the boys who played nearly every night, although not many of them were full-time musicians – they all had day jobs, mostly in the shipyards or on the docks like me.

Every night I'd go home, smarten myself up and head up to the Red Lion or the Bay Horse or about four or five other pubs, and just hang about for a bit. Eventually the bands would gather before heading on to wherever they were playing. More often than not someone was short of a player – but the thing was there were rules, and if you turned up without the right number of guys in your band, you didn't get paid.

So I was the fill-in guy. All I had to do was put the trumpet or clarinet or whatever to my mouth every time the lead guy did, and pretend to play. No one ever knew the difference and, give them their due, the bands all paid me full whack.

There were a few close shaves. The manager of the Marlborough in Shawlands was always suspicious of me. He couldn't prove anything while we were playing but one night before the doors opened he asked me to play a solo. I stood there, thinking about just running for it, when Charlie the bandleader saved me by telling the manager he'd have to pay overtime rates if he wanted us to perform outside the contracted hours! But I never went back to the Marlborough.

It got embarrassing anyway because I started getting a bit of a reputation – Killer Kinnie, they called me, and said I could play in any band in Scotland. In a way they were right!

AL DUNCAN: I used to stand in for a couple of the bands playing in Edinburgh, even though I needed someone to tell me which way up to hold the thing. I won't lie – it all went to my head a bit and I started acting as if I really was a professional musician ... That all changed when I borrowed a trumpet and went to a rehearsal. It was an open rehearsal – I suppose you'd call it a public jam now – where you paid two bob to sit in with whoever turned up. But you never learned anything because you had to play whatever the majority wanted to play, and there was always a group of nearly as many people arguing against it. In the hour I put up with it we played two tunes, with half the band playing it one way and the other half trying to push it another way. I went back to miming – it was much less hassle. But it sorted my ego out.

The Musicians' Union existed to protect the interests of professional players, just like most types of work had their own unions. But they were struggling with the change of times and attitudes. The MU had banned American acts from touring in Britain unless a British act toured the US at the same time, which had led to a dearth of visits from across the Atlantic. Finally an agreement was reached, leading to the arrival of the Count Basie Orchestra in 1954 – a tour which, legend has it, saw dozens of stunned Scottish musicians staggering home to throw their instruments in the bin. More to the point, though, there was an outcry from the music press that the Basie Orchestra weren't using sheet music – they appeared to be busking.

So it wasn't all fun trying to be a musician. Travelling was another issue – if you were fortunate enough to live in a city which still had trams, which were Edinburgh, Glasgow, Aberdeen and Dundee, you could balance the 28-inch bass drum on the gangway beside the driver in many vehicles, and everyone else could pile in and head to the venue. You'd often wind up leaving your gear in the place you played, which could lead to last-moment panic trying to locate someone with keys ahead of a show in a different place. You might find yourself engaged to play a venue and paid in advance, only to find the regular band staging a picket outside, forcing you to become a scab because you'd already spent that night's fee. Then there was simple, downright boredom.

Count Basie

BILL GRACIE: Between 1954 and 1957 I played in the sax section of Laurie Blandford's Band in the Dennistoun Palais. Three or four times every night he would take a little break and I'd trot over to the piano to cover. When I started I used to wonder why some musicians had a reputation for partaking of a wee refreshment. I soon realised the answer was boredom!

You could actually tell the time by the tune the band were playing. In my case 10.10pm was the time for Moonlight Serenade and everything else was pro rata.

While doing my six nights a week in the Palais my girlfriend – who's now my wife of 55 years – went dancing four nights at the Barrowland. I wonder to this day what she got up to ...

The traditional Glasgow holiday trip of going 'doon the watter' was exploding in popularity as more and more people acquired their own transport – in 1953 the car ferry to Bute had eight bookings for the Easter bank holiday, while a year later it had 212. To celebrate its new status as the dance hall for 'Glasgow by the Sea', the Pavilion Ballroom in Rothesay had a new sprung floor fitted. Many such floors were made with bending stretches of wood woven underneath the floorboards to allow bounce which helped with absorbing shock and made dancing easier. Some were even fitted with steel tram springs – or at least, it was claimed they were.

But it's just a coincidence that the slinky toy made its sprung appearance on stairways across the country in the same year. Food rationing ended nine years after the war had, while

Johnny Kennoway and band were a big draw in central Scotland in the 1950s – Edo Brown plays bass on the left

Main photo: The Grove Nicol Orchestra

Insert, left: Dave Marshall and Bill Morrison of the Grove Nicol Orchestra

Insert, above: Bassist Edo Brown, was one of many 'tub' bassists who was forced to find creative ways of carting the huge instrument around during his time with the Grove Nicol Orchestra

Edo Brown plays bass in an 11-piece band of the 1950s

immigration authorities in Canada offered 'an unlimited future – assured jobs and housing' to farmers and farm workers, and 'farms at moderate prices with possible deferred purchase arrangements'. For those who stayed life continued at the dancin'. People leaned against the wall smoking cinnamon sticks, trying to look as cool as James Dean was about to look in the movie *Rebel Without A Cause*.

ADAM KEITH: Cinnamon sticks ... why did we do it? It was usually because a foreign boat had sailed into Aberdeen full of sailors who knew Embassy cigarette coupons weren't British money, meaning we couldn't fool them into swapping coupons for fags ... The Beach Ballroom really stank some nights – tobacco and cinnamon smoke don't mix, I can tell you.

FRANK FERRI: I was in the merchant navy and my ship would return to Leith on the Sunday, usually at midnight. So I went to the Rooms on Monday and Tuesday, despite the fact my ship sailed again at 11pm on the Tuesday night. That resulted in my first pier-head jump, and I'm sure I'm not alone.

I'd asked a girl that had taken my eye if I could see her home, having carefully checked out her geography. Not her figure – I'd already done that – but where she lived, hoping it wasn't as far away as Granton, for example. I was in luck: it was only a few hundred yards from the dance hall.

So after a bit of innocent necking, as you do, I realised I'd left myself too little time to go home, get my kit and get to my ship. I ran to my house then on down to the docks, where of course the ship could not have been berthed further away. I reckon it was a total distance of a mile from my house. When I entered the dock gates, I heard my ship blowing off her horn. She was bow out and about to release her afterspring. I threw my wee case aboard to a deck hand then I made a jump of about five feet.

If I'd mistimed the jump I'd have been chewed up by the propeller – but I landed safe and sound. Praying the skipper hadn't seen me, I went straight to my cabin and hit the sack. Ah – young love!

Light up: cinnamon sticks

GLEN ELLIOT: Every Saturday night a large bunch of apprentices from Babcock and Wilcox in Renfrewshire would venture to the Dennistoun Palais. You had to be early to join the queue, then you had the opportunity to join in the banter.

One of us, Big AB, who was of course really quite small, was late for everything – one night he was very late and had difficulty getting into the queue beside us.

People were giving him stick for trying to jump in so he came out with the excuse: 'I'm late because I couldnae get the pins oot o' mah new shirt!' He was immediately relegated to the back of the queue.

Another night we were chatting up a group of girls by actually talking about birds, the kind that fly. We were asking if they'd ever seen pigeons, sparrows, chaffinches and so on.

A girl, obviously from Newton Mearns, arrived late and only got the tail-end of the conversation. But she was eager to join in, so when one of us asked: 'Have you got blue tits?' she replied: 'No, no – we have central heating!'

3 I hit the town with my Old Spice, Lucky Strike and a Zippo lighter

GREATER communication across the Atlantic had opened Scotland's ears to new music, including the rock'n'roll which was beginning to make an impression in via Elvis' 'That's All Right Mama', Bill Haley's 'Crazy Man, Crazy' and Big Joe Turner's 'Shake, Rattle And Roll' and an increasing number of follow-ups.

FRANK FERRI: The right-hand side in front of the Palais stage was considered the Yankee corner, where the Americans from Kirknewton airbase would congregate and attract the bottled-blondes looking to marry a Yank for a better life in the States – much to the envy and anger of the local lads. Generally speaking, if a local lad asked these girls to dance, they got a knock back. After a 12-month trip to the United States during my merchant navy days I had developed an American accent that I could slip into quite comfortably. Dressed in the clothes I'd bought in America, I could pull the birds in this disguise easily. I had some Old Spice too – all we usually had was Imperial Leather, and leather was exactly what it smelled like. I hit the town with a liberal spray of Old Spice to my face, a packet of Lucky Strike cigarettes and a Zippo lighter in my pocket. Unfortunately I can't detail the results it produced in a family publication ...

Once again change was very much on the cards, although no one knew what that change would be. In the end, it came to Scotland from England rather than the USA – although it was caused by a Scotsman. Lonnie Donegan was a member of Chris Barber's jazz band when he decided to make use of some recording time which had been booked and paid for, but wasn't needed. He grabbed a banjo and recorded rough versions of what he called 'American folk music': simple songs with a few basic chords that almost anyone could play.

It became known as skiffle music and Donegan became known as the founding father of pop. But Lonnie wasn't trying to found anything. He once said: 'In Britain we were separated from our folk music tradition centuries ago, and we were given the idea that music was for the upper classes. They said you had to be clever to play music. When I came along with three old chords people thought if I could do it, so could they. They were right – it was the reintroduction of folk music.'

The result was the skiffle craze as guitar sales in the UK soared from 50,000 in 1950 to over 200,000 five years later. Suddenly, all over Scotland kids were making basses from tea-chests, drumkits from washboards and putting simple ditties together. And even more astonishingly, they were being paid to do it.

ROY KITLEY: When I was 15 I set up the Pythons Skiffle Group. We cribbed the name from the Vipers, one of the big groups of the time. We were kept really busy with cinema gigs, church socials, parties and dances. It really did happen overnight and suddenly there were thousands of groups, sometimes several in one street, and the rivalry was pretty fierce.

Roy Kitley's Pythons were in demand from the moment they formed the band in school

PETE AGNEW: Long before we were Nazareth I formed the Spitfires with some mates from school. We borrowed their big brothers' acoustic guitars and I sang. You couldn't really hear anything because it was acoustic guitars on stage. I could sing the tune so I just ignored the guitarists and sang 'That'll Be the Day'.

There was these young guys from Kirkcaldy – one of them was playing chords and I thought, 'That's what it's supposed to sound like! I'm going to get a guitar and learn how to do that.' So I got one and began learning ... I was mucking about and I started finding chords – a G, then a C, then a D, and I called them one, two, three and so on.

Later I was playing with my mate who'd been to guitar lessons. I was saying, 'Play a three,' and he was saying, 'What are you talking about? That's a D!'

He showed me this chord book where it was all there, telling you how to do it. I could have worked it all out in a week! Talk about young and stupid! We still muck about in the dressing room – 'Play a four!' That's an E, by the way.

Elsewhere in the UK, a young man by the name of Lennon put together a skiffle group called the Quarrymen, while a lad called Reg Dwight began enjoying his piano playing more as he listened to skiffle, and a kid named Brian May decided to invest in a guitar. But the vast majority of that musical outpouring was still amateurish and haphazard – so who was listening to it? That new invention: the teenager. Spurred on by the American influence

Bill Haley and his Comets had been playing the circuit for some years before they exploded with the rock'n'roll revolution. Right, a British poster from an early 1960s tour, by which time Haley's star was on the wane

teenagers were inventing their own scene, their own way of talking, and even their own way of dressing.

ANDY DUFF: The first time I got a Teddy boy suit I couldn't wait to get fronted up to Stewart's. But I was met at the door by the owner, who in no uncertain manner made it clear no bloody Teds were going to be allowed in. Being a big-mouth, I said: 'Stuff your old dance rules – we'll go to the Cavendish instead'. He told us he'd give us five pounds if we managed to get in, so off we went ... and we did get in! We went back and the owner did give us the fiver. You could say that was the start of Teddy boys at Stewart's – and we fitted in fine.

Soon after that night a redheaded girl came in. Man, she was gorgeous and well stacked – did she turn heads! It was quite fun to see the boys racing to get the first dance with her. Believe it or not, at the time she didn't really interest me ... but I bet my mates two and six that when the first ladies' choice was announced, she'd ask me.

Sure enough, that's what happened. You should have seen the looks on my mates' faces. Little did they know she lived round the corner from me and I was just about the only familiar face in the room. Little did I know she would wind up being Mrs Jean Duff!

COLIN DUNCAN: I couldn't have cared less about the bands in the town hall at Huntly – and I wasn't the only one. The band played from about half past eight until nine then half past nine until ten, and chucking-out time was about half ten. But while the band was on the floor was half-empty because people were away getting a cup of tea or whatever. It all changed when the band came off and the DJ came on, though – because nine until half-nine was 'action time' where they played all the smoochy numbers. The lights would go down and you'd get yourself a partner as soon as possible, then you'd go for a break again at half-nine when the band came back, ready to get into action again at ten – and not very often with the same partner.

For the first time an age group had its own fashion sense. The Teddy boys would be followed later by mods and rockers, hippies, punks, metalheads, goths and many more. But in the late 50s it was everyone's aim to style your hair in the duck's-arse quiff, slip on a bootlace tie and maybe – just maybe – own a Vauxhall Cresta.

Sadly, with all the pent-up emotion and energy from a new wave of kids whose parents didn't understand them, violence was bound to come into the story. If you take it in the context of how many thousands of people were suddenly out at the dancin' compared to how many had been there in the past, it doesn't seem too incredible. If you also take into account how many communities were meeting who had never met before, it seems even more understandable.

But that was without the intervention of the press, who couldn't refuse the opportunity to write sensational headlines. After the 1953 murder of John Beckley in London by a group of young men the papers labelled Teds, the stories continued, 'Edwardian suits, dance music and a dagger!' *'A Teddy boy stabbed a barber outside his shop with an 18-inch meat knife after the barber asked a group to move away from his shop.' 'Four boatloads of Teddy boys took up action stations on the lake last night when a 25-strong rival gang formed boarding parties ashore. The youths scattered as three squad cars arrived.' 'I witnessed a gory razor fight between two Teddy boys in a crowded park – at least a hundred youths and adults flocked to enjoy the 'fun' yet not a hand was raised to stop the battle until one boy fell to the ground almost unconscious.'*

The Blackboard Jungle, billed as 'the most startling movie in years', was attached to the Edwardian fashion movement as a vicar told the *Daily Mirror*: 'The Teddy boy has no allegiance to party, class or workmates, or to a society that is too complex for him. He has retreated into a private world. He takes the Welfare State for granted. His mind is doped and his instincts stimulated by the illusions of the cinema.' The holy man ended by observing they needed more vitamin C.

In Scotland two particular headlines serve as examples of how things weren't quite the way the papers said: 'Riot at town hall' and 'Battle of Wallyford' – one of which was completely made up, and one which only took on some truth because its publication made it happen.

BILL ALLISON: Paisley Town Hall was always a favourite with us. Band night was usually Saturday – Jimmy McCracken was a regular – and there was a talent contest every Sunday. That Sunday we had the Ricky Barnes All Stars playing instead.

The hall was all seated except for a space between the front rows and the stage – all the girls used to crowd in there to dance. It had been raining so there were handbags and umbrellas placed on the stage. The hall manager wasn't bothered about all the stuff being put on the stage – it was being *placed* there, not thrown. The bouncers and the bands weren't bothered either.

The All Stars were great. They did a song called 'Skin Deep' which had a drum solo, and like many bands to this day, the rest of the musicians went off stage while the drummer did his bit. They came back on, finished the set, everyone clapped, and that was that.

Next day I picked up the paper and saw the headline 'Riot at Town Hall' across the front page. The article went on about items being thrown onto the stage, but the nearest thing to that was all the umbrellas and bags that had been placed on stage. Then it said the band had walked off in disgust, when they'd just gone off during the drum solo.

The story about a riot always bothered me – it just wasn't true, and it reflected badly on the people of Paisley. I suppose it must have been a publicity stunt, or maybe just a really quiet day for the paper. But it just didn't happen.

STEWART CAMPBELL: One Sunday night at Wallyford Miners' Club I was dancing with a girl and someone asked for an excuse-me dance. It was a done thing in those days, although you weren't supposed to keep doing it to the same couple. This guy had done it to me twice but I wasn't looking for any bother.

Stewart Campbell

Someone who'd been watching came up to me and said, 'Has he just cut in again?' and when I said he had, all hell broke loose.

I've no idea why ... I think it must have just been an excuse to get the guy, whoever he was. It turned into a massive fight but it was soon stopped by the bouncers. I remember one called Curly who kept the peace very well. We all went home and it was forgotten about – so we thought.

The next Thursday there was a fight at the Edinburgh Palais and my head was split open after a bouncer threw a chair. It had no connection with what had happened at Wallyford. It was just bad luck, that's all.

But then the paper ran a story about an Edinburgh gang planning to go to Wallyford that Sunday to avenge my injury. It was crazy – there just wasn't any truth – but that's what the paper said. They had a line like 'Gangs from Edinburgh are going to avenge gang leader Stew Campbell.' They even went to a café in the Kirkgate to interview some guys, and told him we were called the OMO Gang because we always wore clean white shirts. They even printed that!

'OMO Gang' fashion

And because it was in the paper, loads of guys got organised from Leith to go to Wallyford that Sunday. But Willie Merilees had police waiting everywhere. So when the battle started they came in and arrested almost everybody, and they were all charged at Edinburgh court in the High Street.

'Wee Willie Merilees' is a legendary character in Scottish policing. After showing immense bravery as a young man they changed the rules for him because he was shorter than regulation height, and by the time he retired he was a much-decorated chief constable. Along with single-handedly defeating the Teddy boy menace, as celebrated in a comic book of a few years later, he also broke up spy rings, caught murderers and set up a Christmas charity fund for the children of men he'd put in jail. One legend even has him pretending to be a baby in a pram in order to catch a suspect at Waverley Station.

But an Edinburgh firm of tailors pointed out: 'We sell long draped jackets, narrow trousers, "slim jim" ties, shirts with cut-away buttoned-down collars and whatever the modern youth wants. Our business is sufficiently big to mean that if all our young customers were hooligans, the City of Edinburgh would require a police force double its current size.'

There's no doubt that violence was a part of the new culture. It was scary for some people from nice areas, but to other people it really was just a way of life and part of the night out.

DAVE QUINN: I can honestly only remember one fight in the dancin' in Glasgow back then, and I was out four or five nights a week, so I'm not sure it was as common as people say it was. But it was big fight, right enough – there were a big lot of Yanks down from Dunoon and they were dancing in the Locarno. A girl refused a dance from a Glasgow guy, and in those days you were meant to sit out the dance if you'd told a guy 'no'. Next thing a Yank asked her to dance and she went straight up. It just kicked off – the Glasgow guys had had enough. I left before it got really heated up, but everyone was talking about it for days afterwards.

JOHN CLARKE: In those days there were Teddy boys and there were Edwardians – both names are derived from the same source but the two styles were different in so many ways. Teddy boys were seen as boisterous, sometimes unfriendly, sometimes in large unruly groups, who were not generally accepted too well by the older generation. In contrast the Edwardians were dandy-boys, although they knew how to dress. They chose the best quality material and your suit took eight weeks to be made. In Edinburgh the Teddy boys used Jacksons in Leith Street while Edwardian young men favoured Burtons. Mind you, there were many great guys who were Teddy boys – so the few made a bad name for the many.

CHRISTINE DOHERTY: I remember the first Teddy boys appearing round the town in Kirkcaldy. You were supposed to ignore them but they looked so smart, and even though I suppose we were a bit naive there *was* something attractive about all that posing.

It was a few months before they were allowed into the Burma Ballroom – they wouldn't have been let in at all except there hadn't been any trouble in town since the fashion arrived. I'll admit we were a bit wild-eyed that first Saturday night when the Teds came in and started looking round the room. But I decided to take a leaf out of their book and act as if nothing bothered me.

One of them came right up towards me and I hoped I was still looking as if butter wouldn't melt. I didn't know what he was going to say but I didn't expect: 'Hey, are you lookin' for a boyfriend? Or a manfriend?'

I burst out laughing – and he started laughing straight after as well. In the end we had a great night and I saw him again a few times. He could really dance and he really did look smart.

A particularly inaccurate dramatisation of the Wallyford episode from *Valiant* comic

4 Free plays on the jukebox with a nail file, Bovril and fags for tuppence each

HOT on the heels of skiffle came the full breakthrough of America's biggest-ever export: rock'n'roll. Bill Haley and the Comets had hit at the end of 1955 with 'Rock Around the Clock', a few months before Lonnie Donegan's 'Rock Island Line' – but while rock'n'roll took a little time to explode like skiffle had done, it burnt much brighter and for much longer.

Alongside the movie of the same name and its 1957 follow-up 'Don't Knock the Rock', Haley and the American acts laid claim to the new teenager world and its post-war rebellious nature. And although it was a degree more difficult to play than skiffle, it inspired another million fingers to start twiddling strings. It also inspired millions of limbs to try a new dance – jive had arrived.

BARRY McEWAN: I'm not proud of it but my pal Rab and I got our first guitars as the proceeds of crime. We just had to have one each but there was no chance of affording one and with our dads' shady histories no shop in the city would give us them on the never-never.

So we took a new slant on an old screw ... Another pal of ours borrowed his dad's guitar and started busking on a street corner with us clapping along and putting the hat round. When the time was right and someone stopped to put a few pennies in, I dropped some change on the ground. The guy would think it was his own money and bent down to pick it up – and Rab would be into his pockets for whatever he could grab.

It didn't feel that good to know we were stealing from the folk who were giving us money in the first place. All I can tell you is we needed those guitars. If it helps, we went on to run charity fundraisers once we'd got a band together. Is it an apology if you never tell anyone why you're saying sorry? I hope so ...

ROLLIN' JOE: When you went to the Barrowland the first thing you saw was people jiving. It was just in the corner, a place they called Mug's Alley – you had to keep out of the way for people who were doing the older dances. I didn't see the Teds jiving. I saw them jumping about enjoying themselves, but not many of them were any good at dancing. Most of us didn't go about trying to be flash – we were just trying to be smart and learn the jive moves so we could dance and meet girls.

FRANK FERRI: The Assembly Rooms in Leith was open six days a week. If you went on Monday you were given a ticket to get back in free on the Tuesday. The Rooms had a strict rule: no rock'n'roll bands. You danced to Alexander and his Band, a seven-piece unit without a guitar in sight, and jiving was not allowed. That was primarily because it interrupted those who wanted to dance traditionally.

Nevertheless, if an appropriate tune was played you'd do a wee jive in the corner, keeping your eye out for any bouncers. The problem was that if you were good at it you'd soon attract a wee crowd around you, clapping with encouragement. That would draw the attention of the stewards who immediately asked you to leave and barred you until such time as they saw fit to let you back in. It happened to me once and it broke my heart getting turned away every night for three months – all just for jiving.

Reports abounded of 'hooliganism' during showings of 'Rock Around The Clock', although in reality people just didn't want to sit still when they heard the music. A psychiatrist was asked if rock'n'roll, described in the same press article as a 'weird and disturbing new form of jazz', simply appealed to basic sex instincts and replied: 'Of course it does – most music and dancing does that. It certainly doesn't cause rioting.'

Nevertheless, in many parts of the country jiving remained banned, as did rock'n'roll bands. In Dundee, for example, Andy Lothian and his Band offered Saturday afternoon dancing for two shillings and Saturday evening for five shillings, and later added 'A special night for over-20s to enjoy orthodox dancing in a happy atmosphere – no jiving and no teenagers' all for five bob. Around the same time Dundee's JM Ballroom was one of the venues around the country running local heats for the Miss Great Britain National Bathing Contest. The top prize was £1000 with the heat prize £20 and a week's holiday in Morecambe. That came after the JM's Marilyn Monroe Wiggle Contest – so effort was being put in to keep the crowds from moving over to rock'n'roll.

But it wasn't going to work.

RONNIE SIMPSON: Miss Dunn, our music teacher, told me: 'Simpson, we're doing a great work by Gilbert and Sullivan. *Pirates of Penzance* will see that trashy music of yours dead and buried in a matter of weeks. I will give you a simple choice: get back in line with the other policemen in the chorus or leave for your silly short-lived world of rocking and rolling.'

So it was the beauty of strutting the boards with a painted-on moustache in the high school opera singing 'Ta-ran-ta-ra, zing-boom' ... or having a chance – just a *chance* – to sing 'A wop bop-a-lula a wop bam boo'.

I never saw Miss Dunn again.

Meanwhile, the Dounreay experimental nuclear reactor complex began taking shape in the far north of Scotland, causing an influx of up to 30,000 workers from the south, who obviously brought their musical tastes with them. Early among the arrivals were brothers Dave and Bill Fehilly, who came as painters but soon abandoned the work to become full-time promoters.

Their first venture had been the Spot, a coffee bar which introduced the juke box to Caithness – but by the end of the decade they were running live events in the Boys' Brigade Hall in Wick and were soon using the Assembly Rooms as well. And they were playing to an educated audience because Caithness could listen to the US forces' radio network as well as Radio Luxembourg, so they were spoilt for rock'n'roll choice.

The Fehillys knew about putting on a show – they brought the big-name acts to play, but they had local outfits as the support acts, which made sure the tickets sold (if there had been any doubt they wouldn't). They ran theme nights like pyjama parties and offered giveaways like pairs of tights for the first ten girls to arrive.

They were responsible for putting Wick on the rock'n'roll map and fostered local acts like the Aktual Fakts, the Federals and the Rhythm Four.

A 17-inch TV set cost 67 guineas or 11s a week rental. The Campaign for Nuclear Disarmament was founded days after the UK said it would retaliate in the event of a Soviet missile assault. *Melody Maker* splashed the headline '*Pop rot – call a halt now!*' and also demanded an end to the promotion of rock'n'roll, with a newspaper journalist complaining, '*Artistry has been kicked out of the stage door and performers who can provide ephemeral thrills are taking its place.*'

Incidentally, the jukebox had been around for a while but hadn't really taken off because of expense and licensing problems. By the mid-50s they were very much in vogue. In 1945 there had been less than 100 in the UK, but by 1958 there were over 13,000 stationed in cafés, offering the opportunity to meet someone against an exciting musical backdrop before you went up the dancin'.

CAMMIE WEIR: They were great evenings in Dunoon, meeting up in Drovandi's before heading to the Queen's Hall. You could get free plays from the jukebox by poking it with a nail file. You could have a cup of Bovril on cold nights for sixpence and old Mama Drovandi would sell you single fags for tuppence each.

DENNIS BRUCE: My pal Frank was a shy lad of a serious disposition. He was taking his first steps into the gallus world of tripping the light fantastic in the

Glasgow Locarno – but his knowledge of the opposite sex was limited. He had no sisters and he attended a single-sex school. Hearing the girls liked a good conversation on the dance floor he decided to leave nothing to chance, and primed himself on the topics of the day.

The fateful evening came and out went Frank in his best bib and tucker. After watching a few dances he settled his eye on a lovely little brunette in a floral frock. It took him a few more dances to pluck up his courage, but as the band struck up a lively tune he strode forward and asked her to dance.

They took to the floor and soon Frank felt it was time to launch into his repertoire. The subject of the CND had been in the news that week so he decided to start there – to which his partner stopped dead in her tracks and said: 'What Christmas cracker did you come out of?' and flounced off the floor.

Frank learned then and there that the art of conversation on the dance floors of Glasgow depended less on highflown sentiments and more on banter.

FRANCES LYTTLE: When you wanted to avoid American servicemen at the dancin' my parents' advice worked a treat – you wore a little plastic CND badge on your dress. Sure enough, they steered clear when they saw it!

JIMMY HOWISON: The Concert Hall in Troon was a very good-looking place which opened on Saturday nights. A problem for the local lads is we had to compete with the soldiers from the army camp at Dundonald. We didn't even bother going to Bobby Jones' in Ayr a lot of the time because the girls who went there were looking for a Yank from Prestwick. But the biggest problem at the Concert Hall was trying to get on the last bus at 11.30pm – there never seemed to be enough buses and for some of us it could be a long walk home.

The Moorings at Largs was considered up-market – entry on a Saturday night was seven and six compared to the two and six of most places. So the shipyard boys of Ardrossan and the explosives workers of Stevenston didn't frequent it! Instead we went to the Castle Craigs at Ardrossan, which was so popular you'd have queues forming from early evening. It was a town council event and the Clyde Valley Stompers used to play there all the time. But it literally emptied overnight – I think people just got fed up queuing for it. On Monday nights we had the Caledonian Hall in Irvine which was also very busy, but it was very much a local scene. Midweek we had Brown's Merrymakers at the Recreation Club at Nobel's explosives in Stevenston.

If Caithness had the Fakts and the Federals and the Four, Aberdeen had the Alligators and

The Clyde Valley Stompers with Peter Kerr, foreground right, enjoyed the trad jazz boom with TV and movie appearances

the Rockefellers, Dundee had Mark Drayton and the Hounds and the Sound Four, Montrose had the Blackhawks, Dunfermline had the Red Hawks, Glasgow had Ricky Barnes and his All Stars plus a number of Alex Harvey Bands – and all over the country the real revolution was beginning to take form. If you knew where to look you could always find the old guard – or a new fashion you weren't expecting.

KEVIN DORRIAN: My dad, Danny Dorrian, was a very-well known piano player around Edinburgh from the early 1940s until his death in 1995. He played everywhere – the Palais, the West End Café, the Imperial Hotel, the Caledonian and so on. But he's best remembered for his 14-year residency as musical director at the Maybury Roadhouse, when the dinner-dance was very much in vogue. He started in 1955 and stayed until 1969 and it was mobbed every night. All the way through the rock'n'roll era there were queues on a Friday and Saturday to see the Danny Dorrian Quintet.

STEWART CAMPBELL: I used to go to the Dumbarton Burgh Hall around 1957 with a girlfriend. I couldn't believe it – when the dancing started all the girls were on one side of the room and the men opposite. You had to meet in the middle of the floor to ask someone to dance, then you had to dance in an eternal circle. Then someone in the band would shout: 'Charlie Tully!' and all the Celtic fans would cheer, followed by: 'Willie Waddell!' and the Rangers fans would cheer. I thought it was very weird.

STEWART ALEXANDER: The Burntisland Palais attracted an older clientele so people in my age group went to the dancin' in Dunfermline. You had to get to the Kinema early if you wanted to get in. One night the band announced: 'The next dance will be a mambo'. At the time Perez Prado had a big hit. Silence fell and a lad close to me turned to the person next to him and said: 'How the hell dae ye dae the mambo?' For some reason I always remember that story ...

If there really had been rock'n'roll riots in Scotland before, they were about to be replaced by a completely different kind of crowd scene. The era of the bona fide rock star arrived in the shape of two particular big names, and they both discovered the real end of stardom when they came north of the border.

Tommy Steele was the icon of the new age but nearly abandoned his career after a visit to Dundee in 1958. The papers reported of his Caird Hall show: *'With two choruses to go in Mabeline, a song written by Tommy himself, he let out an enthusiastic 'Oh Yeah' and three hundred girls caught the strong body of stewards off guard and mobbed the stage. Fans jumped, in some cases 10 feet, from the organ gallery and cut off Tommy's escape. He was submerged in a sea of screaming girls. Manager Larry Parnes fought his way to Tommy's side. Tommy's right arm had been twisted up his back, his shirt ripped from his back and hair pulled from his head by admirers. The battle for Tommy between the mob and the stewards lasted several minutes. He was pulled almost unconscious to the door leading backstage and collapsed in the passage. The battle on the stage ended when someone momentarily plunged the hall into darkness. After this the audience, with a few exceptions began to file out of the hall. One steward said 'I have never experienced anything like that. I thought he was going to be killed'.*

A year later the ladies of Dundee were at it again, this time with young Cliff Richard in the Gaumont Theatre. *The Courier* reported: *'Two young women lay on the road under the wheels of a private car that was blocking the rock star's taxi. The police, who saw their carefully planned schedule for Richard's exit coming to grief, had to clear a way for his taxi as others in the milling crowd dragged the two girls from under the private car. During Richard's second performance one youth rushed towards the stage, but was turned back by stewards. He was taken to the exit when several more gathered in the aisle to block the way. Two policemen were called from outside and the youths were ejected. During the show it was the same screaming story. Richard's 10 numbers were barely audible above the cries of girls who threw their arms in the air. They pressed forward and the barrier in front of the orchestra pit bent under the strain. A girl had to be lifted bodily when she rushed to the stage. Later crowds gathered outside the Royal Hotel where their idol was staying. Richard's taxi cruised around the city for half an hour to see if they would disperse, but again the police had to clear the way and in the melée a swing door was smashed.'*

It all added up to a heady new mixture of youth and energy – and one of the entertainment industry's biggest tragedies to date would demonstrate just how deeply the world was responding to the new craze.

STEWART CAMPBELL: Jimmy Savile was the guest DJ at the Palais de Dance in Edinburgh. We were talking to him and he noticed my girlfriend was chewing

A standard frenetic evening at the JM Ballroom in Dundee

some gum. He asked if she had any more but she said, 'Only what's in my mouth' – so he took it from her and started chewing it himself!

We'd been jiving to the music of the Big Bopper, Buddy Holly and Ritchie Valens, and as we left the next day's papers were on sale, as was the custom back then. And the headlines were that all three had been killed in a plane crash. The shock was unbelievable to many of us.

GRAHAM POWELL: Hank Williams had died back in 1953 – I think it was drink but no one really said. And I remember his last song, which came out after he was gone, was called 'I'll Never Get out of This Alive', so there you go. But his death didn't hit us the way that plane crash did. And I don't think it was just because a plane crash was amazing all by itself, without Buddy Holly, the Big Bopper and Ritchie Valens. I think everything had changed – they meant so much more to us than the music of Hank Williams. No disrespect to Hank, but in 1953 you liked music. By 1959 you *loved* music and lived for it. It was us who had changed.

DAVID GIBSON: They called it 'the day the music died' and of course it's in Don McLean's 'American Pie'. It's really no exaggeration. I don't think a celebrity death had ever really hit the community like that before. Only a royal death had come close.

It had an upside, though – for about three weeks afterwards I could get a dance with a lassie and then act all upset, and tell her it was because of Buddy Holly. It was good for an extra couple of minutes out the back with her ...

RONNIE SIMPSON: A band called the Cordettes used the Bellshill YMCA for rehearsals and I just loved being there with them, in the company of aspiring rock gods. I should have got the message when I discovered they didn't know the words to the latest hot songs. But I did – so I became unofficial lyric writer. I scribbled down the words from either the radio or the record for our singer Eddie to perform. So at least I was involved in this new wonderful music.

Most of the dates – the word 'gig' hadn't been invented – were at church socials, youth clubs and miners' welfare hops. Soon I was promoted to singing the odd song. I went on and mimicked the artists I'd seen. I did an impression of Gene Vincent doing 'She-She-She Little Shiela', where I threw my leg over the mike and stand, just like Gene. Another popular attempt was 'Running Bear', the Johnny Preston hit, and I always seemed to get to sing the daft Bobby Darin songs like 'Splish Splash'.

In hindsight I was thought of as good for a laugh rather than the future of rock'n'roll ... Luckily it took me many years to realise that or I may have quit with a big rid neck there and then.

Then one night, for reasons I still don't know, Eddie walked off the stage just prior to the start of quite a prestigious gig. I think he left the following day for New Zealand, but who knows for sure – he even left his PA setup. The word 'system' had not been invented either.

With the audience streaming into the hall and the band in mild panic, all eyes fell on me with those comforting words: 'At least you know the lyrics – we'll struggle through'.

And I found myself the lead singer in a rock'n'roll band.

1960s

It wasn't an easy birth ... but with
a twist, a beat and a rock and roll,
the new generation made their
feelings known

SOMETHING TO SHOUT ABOUT

5 What do you want for seven and six ... Rock Hudson?

IF YOU think the world changes fast now you'll be surprised to think about how people were horrified at the pace of change as the 1950s gave way to the 1960s. Just five years previously it had seemed like Scotland could look forward to business as usual in the dance halls for eternity. Then suddenly there'd been rock'n'roll, then skiffle had come and gone, followed by jive dancing elbowing in – and if you were of a certain opinion, the worst was yet to come.

Chubby Checker tore a big hole through the middle of dancing culture when he hit with 'The Twist'. Like many big songs of the day, it had had previous outings before Checker's – but it was his version which became a global hit and introduced a new style of expression: 'Dancing apart to the beat'.

When you think about it, it's crazy ... For years previously you could hold your partner close, with dancing as a contact sport. Suddenly it was no-touchy-touchy except for the slow dances every now and again – and it was preferred.

But then, it was a lot easier to twist than it was to jive or follow the steps of a strict tempo dance. It did for the dancin' what skiffle had done for playing music. If you look at it one way, it gave expression back to the masses. If you look at it another, it spoiled a fine tradition.

ROLLIN' JOE: There were incredible jive clubs all over Glasgow. Dalgleish's, Johnny Wilson's in Cathcart and later in Byres Road too, Bill Murdoch's, the Lindella – which is still going. You paid your money and they taught you to jive. Glasgow jive was unique as well – we had a lot more moves, a lot more soul.

It's important to realise rock'n'roll was a dance culture – it was about a band playing and people dancing. It wasn't really around for long. It was only 1960 or 1961 that ballrooms started taking on what you'd call rock'n'roll groups. There were the Sabres, the Chaperones, the Red Hawks from Dunfermline, and one or two others. Before that it was traditional dance bands who might play a bit of rock'n'roll for the jivers.

And the thing is, rock'n'roll was about real dancing – not just throwing yourself around the room. And you didn't do it on your own either – if you tried dancing on your own the men in white coats would come!

But the twist killed it stone dead. Chubby Checker totally aborted rock'n'roll. After that there were all those other cheap dances from America – and every single one of them was shite.

ALAN URQUHART: I will admit everyone could do the twist and it was the first time you saw the older folk doing a similar dance to us young upstarts. But it was goodbye to a lot of contact dancing and that really was a shame.

ANNE MARIE GREGORY: We loved jiving but loved the twist even more. My boyfriend and I were in Rothesay Pavilion when the record came on and we let loose. The floor cleared – no one had seen the twist before, but they started copying us and the place went wild. I loved that dance – and the clothes we wore when we danced. It was all good clean fun.

FRANK FERRI: It's true that even then we had our share of assholes and villains and a bit of gang warfare. But they kept it to themselves – you could walk the streets safely. Employment was good, we had a wee bit of money to spend with no great ambitions. Three or four pints at the weekend made you high enough to boost your confidence at the dancin'. Guys and gals took the trouble to dress up – you couldn't get into the dancin' without a collar and tie.

We had contact dancing where you took the trouble to have a conversation with your chosen partner for the dance. If you hit it off, you moved to the next stage by asking her to go for a coffee or coke in one of the alcohol-free bars. Then you took the lady home, did a bit of necking in her stairway or wherever and maybe asked for a further date. Guys were no different then – with our hormones working overtime we all had the same object in mind, but quite often that wee encounter ended up in a serious relationship.

ROLLIN' JOE: Bill Haley came to the Barrowland. Bill Haley! I nipped out of work to try to buy tickets, thinking there'd be a big queue. Nothing. Same with the show – you could wander straight in no problem. The room was about quarter full, and only about half a dozen people were jiving. You can say what you like about Bill Haley, but he was rock'n'roll. Seeing him playing to an empty room – well, you knew it was over.

The future was in beat music, it seemed, and the evidence was provided by the rise of the beat clubs which slowly saw the ballrooms' grip on the scene fall away. In Glasgow La Cave

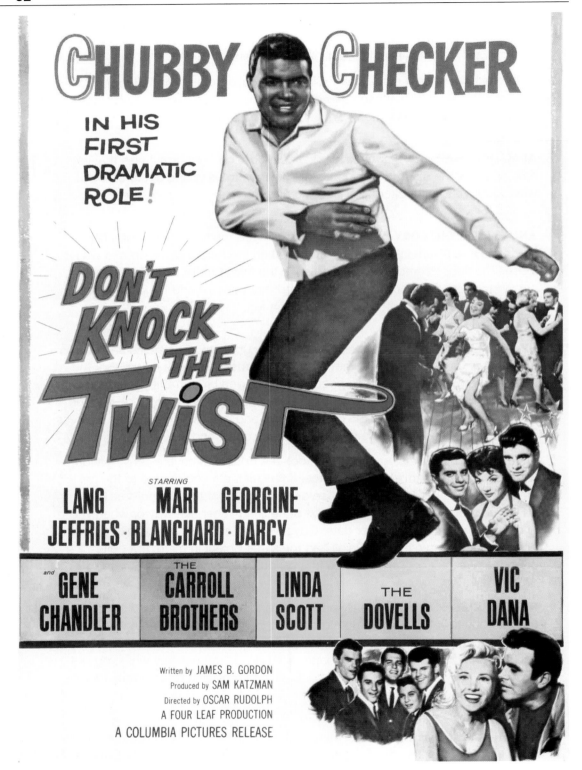

became the city's first all-nighter venue where you could buy dinner, dance the night away then buy breakfast; while in Edinburgh the Waldman brothers opened their first coffee bar which served the beatnik community.

BRIAN NOBILE: Derek Nicol had started a record hop in the Church of Scotland Hall in Rosyth. After a few weeks it had got so busy he was in position to pay for a live group to come in and play. As the weeks went by the audience had got bigger and bigger – and the church elders didn't take kindly to pop music drawing bigger crowds than they were.

So Derek moved to the Co-op Hall, which had been used as a dancin' venue for years. He couldn't get the Friday or Saturday but got the Sunday, and opened on September 4, 1960, as the Stardust Club. The Ricky Barnes All Stars headlined alongside local bandleader Billy Hunter. The first couple of weeks went so well that Derek took up the option of the Wednesday night as well.

When Derek booked Vince Eager there was such a demand for tickets that he decided to book the Kinema Ballroom for the show. That's when the Kinema management were forced to take notice of pop music.

New manager Cecil Hunter had brought the Zephyr Guitar Four in the previous year but there had been an outcry by the old guard. So the Kinema owners set up Ballroom Enterprises, bought over the hire of the St Margaret's Hall and started putting on pop nights.

Jim Brown had already built up a following for his pop nights there so he was furious to be bought over. His Jim Brown Band soon had a strong rivalry with the Top Notchers, which Cecil played in and represented. Brown started running dance nights in other venues so the dancers weren't complaining because they were being treated to a huge array of the biggest names in a huge array of halls.

ARTHUR SCOTT: Your interaction with the dances at the new Strathpeffer Pavilion started long before you ever set foot in the place. The week leading up to a Friday night was filled with anticipation but centred mainly on two things: what you would wear and who you would meet.

I remember being told in no uncertain terms that Cuban heels would not go with bellbottoms. What did I know? And as for who you would meet – well, it was pot luck, but if you were lucky you wouldn't be turned down for a slow dance. Although normally the best you left with was an optimistic anticipation for the following week ...

You found yourself looking up at it because you approached it from the front by way of two short flights of steps and as you got near the front door the sound of the music punched its way out past the bouncers. You would walk over an image of a highland dancer in full tartan regalia, cut like a mosaic into the floor covering, and pay your cash at the double-windowed booth which stood like an island in a stream diverting people left and right into the main ballroom. Tickets were issued from a machine like the ones you'd see at the cinema. And then the full noise would hit you and you'd be in amongst the dancers who would regularly number up to a thousand.

As your eyes got accustomed to the darkness the glitterball overhead would blind you with its flashing lighthouse welcome. The main threat when making your way round the ballroom to the bars was not from the crush of bodies but from the many cigarettes brandished by dancers and onlookers alike.

If you arrived before ten o'clock it would be relatively deserted, since many folks would have got off the buses and decanted into the Strathpeffer Hotel or the Clachan for a drink to save some money against the prices charged in the Pavilion bars. The rush came when those places closed – in order to be ready the staff in the Toddy Bowl bar would set up glasses of whisky on trays stacked four or five high. The beer to ask for was Oranjeboom while many of the lady drinkers would steer away from the usual vodka and lime or Bacardi and coke and ask for a Moscow Mule or a Blue Lagoon.

A good place to go to get away from the crush was the balcony. It had a small bar and toilets. And apart from the Toddy Bowl there was another bar to the left of the stage.

REG REID: My club days started around 1961, mostly at youth clubs attached to churches. You never knew what it was going to be like although we did follow some bands around the city. The Roadsters, Tresspasers and The Seven come to mind. They all played covers and we wasted a lot of time trying to chat up a lass while we were dancing to undanceable songs – 'Let There Be Drums' and 'Telstar' for instance.

BOB LOUDON: Ah, the old Catholic youth club dances – the guy at the door would ask you what colour of vestments the priest had on at Mass, so I could only get in when my Catholic friends told me the correct answer. I even learned a few prayers because sometimes they asked you to recite one before they let you in!

The Spa Pavillion in Strathpeffer, known locally as the Strath

REG REID: We had a youth club at the Kirk Memorial Church in Edinburgh. I was given the task of finding a band for a dance and remember talking about it to Tam Paton there. He suggested Phil and the Flintstones. I hadn't heard them and I had a worrying time before they started – but Phil was a very good singer and went on to have a career in entertainment. I saw him on STV in the 70s.

Soon Edinburgh also had the Place, the Gamp Club and Bungy's, and slowly but surely the local bands who played during the intervals became the headline acts. Jazz musicians looked down on beat performers because the newcomers couldn't read music and relied more on feel – but it didn't seem to matter because that was what the new crowds wanted to hear. It was a classic case of adapt or die.

BRIAN NOBILE: The truth about the Kinema Ballroom in Dunfermline is they kept modern music out of the venue until they had no option. The home of rock'n'roll in the area was St Margaret's Hall in Dunfermline and the Co-op Hall in Rosyth.

The night Derek Nicol brought Vince Eager to the Stardust Club in the Co-op Hall was the night the Kinema realised the pulling-power of rock'n'roll. Before that, if you wanted to see the latest artists it was the Stardust or Jim Brown's nights at St Margaret's. Jim was a bandleader who mixed the modern music with his upbeat older classics.

REG REID: The Waldman Brothers soon had a load of places in Edinburgh. They'd reputedly been forced out of London by the Krays! I went on a few dates with Brian Waldman's au pair but it was too scary to keep going. Walkers, owned by Peter Williamson, was another tense place to visit. But

Grantown Football Club

Proudly Presents by Public Demand

JIMMY WILSON

AND HIS

MELOTONES

the Band with the BIG reputation

FEATURING

Bert Mackay & His Rocking Guitar

and the BAND within a BAND

The DODO ROSS Trio

to play for *DANCING* in the

VICTORIA INSTITUTE, GRANTOWN

ON

Thursday, May 26

from 9.30 p.m. until 1.30 a.m.

ADMISSION - 4s

Bus leaves Aviemore at 8.30 via Boat of Garten, Nethy-
bridge and Dulnain Bridge

The Melotones before the tragic accident which killed bandleader Jimmy Wilson, shown playing piano, left

Fife's finest: Horace DeMarco and band, above, plus Mike Sata and the Hellcats, below

Fife's finest continued: the impressively-coloured Red Hawks, above, and the Zephyr Guitar Four, below

my formative days at the dancing were spent at the Place – I was there all weekend, sleeping all day and dancing all night. It was a fantastic atmosphere and Sunday night was the best, with the same faces every week and quality bands playing in the lowest cellar.

FRANCES LYTTLE: I was at the Locarno one Saturday night with my friend Ethel. We thought the talent was not so good and we decided to head off, but just then a boy asked Ethel to dance. She took one look at him and refused, to which he quickly replied: 'What do you want for seven and six ... Rock Hudson?' Seven and six was the entry fee for the night – that's how good the patter was at the dancin'.

I used to wear a very tight, straight, black dress with a deep V at the back, which my mother made for me, or a full floral skirt with loads of underskirts and a blouse. And very high-heeled shoes, of course!

Meanwhile, the young gentleman would be wearing his hair longer than he had in the 50s with high-collared button-down shirts, narrow ties, boots with pointed toes and high Cuban heels and shiny mohair suits with tight-bottomed trousers. The jacket would be in the Italian three-button 'bumfreezer' style with cloth-covered buttons.

But if the ballrooms weren't going to allow the new bands in, there were other solutions to be delivered by new figures.

RONNIE SIMPSON: Promoters then were a raggle-taggle bunch – and not always legitimate. Johnny Wilson was my 'move into the big-time'. He was the owner of a private bus company, so he could ship dancers anywhere that he had a hop. One time we had a transport problem and Johnny helped us out, because he was stuck without a band if we didn't get to the venue.

Afterwards he insisted we leave all of our equipment overnight in his garage and collect it the next day. That didn't suit my guys, who were still paying-up the gear. It was my job to tell Mr Wilson I needed his guarantee that everything would be safe.

Mr Wilson slipped on his black gloves as his personal security man left the office, and explained to me just how things would be protected. If I, a 'scatty wee bastard', doubted his word, 'all your shitty stuff' would be kicked into the Clyde.

Not yet getting the reasoning behind the gloves – it stops strike marks showing on body parts – I explained why, with no disrespect to him or his offer, I was anxious that he took care of the boys' gear. He took off his gloves, shook my hand and gave me his *word*. He was as good as that word. He was a good, fair promoter.

The Alex Harvey Soul Band rehearsing ahead of winning over another crowd, if not another support band

Johnny Wilson ran a bus company. Albert Bonici ran a café in Elgin, Bert Ewen was an Aberdeenshire baker, Duncan McKinnon was a Borders farmer and the Fehilly Brothers, first in Thurso then in Dunfermline, ran venues.

We first came across the Alex Harvey Big Soul Band through the Fehillys. They were on at Whitburn Welfare when we arrived from Larbert. We thought we were big time – then we met this older, more experienced crowd of musicians. The first welcome came in the shape of an old-time pewter drinking jug, which you balanced on your arm then aimed for your mouth. It would have been okay if it had been full of diluted spirit like vodka and coke or whisky and coke, or anything and anything. But not with Alex Harvey.

So when we got on stage after that warm welcome following hours on the road without real food, I think it's fair to say we did not go down too well – and it took me years to get the band back into Whitburn Welfare.

Contemporary acts claim that was a standard Harvey ploy to make support bands look bad and get them the shove while the Soul Band kept their bookings. But in that place, at that time, Alex Harvey need not have worried. He suited those audiences perfectly. He was pissed, they were pissed, they got the support band pissed and everybody had a great time.

PETER KERR: The Clyde Valley Stompers did a gig in the Place in Edinburgh – it was a series of old tea warehouses – and there was us upstairs with the Alex Harvey Band downstairs. We were playing different parts of the club, and I remember going down the stairs and hearing what they were doing – it was fantastic! Absolutely bloody shit hot! There was no way we could go that far, but jazz has its roots in blues so we could certainly touch on the rhythm and blues side.

BERT MacKAY: After Bob Hunter joined the Harry Shore Orchestra in the Caledonian Hotel, Inverness, I was asked to come to a Melotones rehearsal in Dingwall. For a young guy like me – I was 20 – it was great to be playing with a band like that. I spent two and a half years with them.

I was very impressed with Jimmy Wilson of the famous Dingwall Wilson brothers. He was a professional no matter what he played, even if it was one of those dumb songs from the 50s or 60s – and there were plenty of them. Jimmy made sure we had all the music for the popular stuff, because the public were always right even if it was dumb. He made sure our rhythms were tight and we played according to the sheet music. We got so popular we even had people who came to listen to us at rehearsals in Dingwall Town Hall.

The night we played the Legion in Invergordon was the night of Jimmy's accident, and an event I'll never forget. We had a full band bus and extra folks who'd come to see us so they were split across the bus and three other vehicles. The roads were very icy that night so it was good not to have the bus cramped with too many people in one vehicle.

Jimmy was in a car in front of the bus, driven by our friend Doreen. Our bus driver (also called Jimmy) kept a constant eye on them until we followed them round a corner and he said, 'Where's the car?' It had crashed into a tree – Doreen had lost control at around 40mph in the ice, which was so bad you could hardly stand up.

I had some medical training so I did what I could. Doreen had a fractured pelvis and cuts from the windscreen and another passenger had a fractured pelvis and broken leg. We pulled Jimmy from the wreck and carried him to a nearby farmhouse, where he lay curled in the foetal position. I realised he'd been injured internally and although we couldn't say how bad he was, I knew it was serious.

An ambulance took them to Raigmore Hospital in Inverness but Jimmy was so serious they took him by plane to Glasgow and operated straight away. He lasted about nine days although it felt like one long day, and I was there when he took his last breath.

For some reason there were a lot of deaths around Dingwall at that time – bus-driver Jimmy said God had taken a holiday. The funeral was huge and we received good wishes from all over the country.

Doreen took a long time to recover because she blamed herself, but the truth was a lot of cars had come off the road over that icy weekend, and there wasn't much gritting at the time.

Jimmy was a wonderful man who made us all happy and I'll never forget him.

Tragically the Blues Council would suffer a similar hell two years later. They lost singer Fraser Calder and bassist James Giffen, and the remaining members split up, leaving one single, 'Baby Don't Look Down', as a hint to how big and successful they could have been.

MICHAEL MacRAE: Wayne Fontana of the Mindbenders liked a drink and seemed to like it more than usual when they played in Aberdeen. He ended up in a bar near the Beach Ballroom drinking with our local rising star Sonny Pearce, who was probably a better singer than Fontana – we all thought so anyway. For some reason Fontana decided to kick off, but before the talk went on very long Sonny picked him up and really gave him a working-over. Sonny was a really nice guy but he could look after himself and Wayne Fontana was well out of order.

What made it worse was when he was picked up off the bar-room floor and dusted down, Fontana was told: 'Not only did he beat the blue hell out of you – he sings your songs better than you do as well!'

ARTHUR SCOTT: The music in the early days at the Strath had been provided on a Saturday night by local dance bands like the Ambassadors, the Melotones and the Strathpeffer Dance Band. But as pop music got going, touring bands from the west and south of Scotland began to make an appearance, including Johnny Law and the MI5, Johnny Little and the Giants and the Chaperones. They played with support on a Friday, then usually on their own at the shorter Saturday dances.

Friday dances were advertised to start at 9pm but rarely got going till after 10. In order to be granted a late licence, each dance was sponsored by a local club, which allowed them to go on till 1.30am.

The Pavilion also hosted the record-breaking Highland Cabaret which ran for 17 years starting in 1962. It showcased local talent on Mondays, Wednesdays and Thursdays and aimed to provide a lively continental atmosphere in the village. Later on, the Tuesday Show was added to complement the Highland Cabaret by giving visitors and locals a different type of entertainment.

There's a valuable lesson to be learned from the Lennoxbank Hotel in Balloch. Loch Lomondside wasn't exactly dead-centre on the dancin' map, but when the owners of the hotel decided to build a new ballroom, they needed to make sure it paid for itself – so there wasn't any time for the idea, 'This is how we've always done it'. Money talked. And money was in beat music.

Like the surprise hit of Vince Eager in Fife, the first night of the new Lennoxbank was a shock success. It had been hired by a rowing club to hold its annual fundraising dance. They'd booked the Apaches from Glasgow and two more of the biggest and newest beat bands – and the result was a phenomenal sellout.

On the back of that one night, the Lido, as it came to be known, turned into a place of pilgrimage, with people from all over the central belt hiring buses and heading to Balloch to see bands they could often see much closer to home.

The rowing club made their annual fundraisers into monthly fundraisers and were soon the best-equipped organisation in Scotland. The Lido, as it came to be known, had the distinction of having a river directly beyond the fire escape – meaning that if you incurred the wrath of a steward you'd also receive a good soaking into the bargain.

ARCHIE YOUNG: I became a bouncer at the Cavendish in Edinburgh. You didn't get trouble often, but when you did it wasn't always where you expected it.

One night a fight broke out in the ladies' toilet. One of the lads went to go in, but we told him to leave it. He ignored us – he went in, and one of the women hit him on the head with a stiletto heel. He had to be rushed to hospital with the heel sticking out of his head.

Some women used to have metal combs with a handle like a tail which was sharpened like a knife with a real point at the end. They'd bring them in for their boyfriends to use. Eventually we had to search all handbags for weapons.

But at least there were never any drugs involved. The only ones I knew of at the time were the purple hearts, which were called 'uppers'. The pop groups used them because it kept them going for days.

The only real problem we had was during the Glasgow fortnight. I was surprised at the Glaswegians because some of the tradesmen I met during my apprenticeship were from Glasgow, and they'd all been really nice blokes and very funny. The satisfaction I got was meeting people and trying to get on with them – if I was involved in a fight or had to eject someone forcibly it put a damper on my night, I could never understand how wicked some people could get.

RONNIE SIMPSON: My stint as a rock'n'roll singer didn't last long. Firstly, I was not a great singer. I might argue on style, but ... Secondly, there was another local band, The Midlanders Combo, who called a meeting.

They were rougher and readier than we were. They'd set off for the wild life in Hamburg and ended up in jail in Wales for stealing food. I never could equate heading for Hamburg with Wales – but they wanted to amalgamate the two bands. So the Cordetted and the Midlanders Combo merged into a lineup complete with two drummers.

Actually all they wanted was our two guitarists, who were, for the time, quite superb. So they kept the Midlanders Combo name – and they kept me too. I wasn't singing but I didn't quit that easily no matter how hard they tried. Although, to be honest, they didn't try too hard. This was my first lesson about musicians – they're really lazy bastards and if they can find a numpty to do the paperwork and get the gigs, who gives a shit?

So started a band that came third in a poll of regulars at the Two Red Shoes in Elgin. Second were Russ Dainty and the Saints. First were the Beatles.

Ah yes – the Beatles ...

6 You didn't need a book of dance steps or to wear your Sunday best

THERE were four of them but they weren't fab just yet. They were just off the plane from their stint in Hamburg and their very first duty was a tour of Scotland. It was supposed to start on January 2 but the powerful winter put paid to that – and that's how the Two Red Shoes put Elgin in the pop history books.

The Beatles had been the Silver Beetles, touring band for Johnny Gentle, on their previous trip north of the border. They'd played but hadn't really turned heads. And as it happened, even although the word 'Beatlemania' was less than 300 days away from entering the language, the band didn't really turn heads on their last pre-fame tour.

> **KEN McNAB:** It was their first appearance in Scotland with Ringo Starr and it was also Ringo's first performance north of the border. Their act was much more polished than in previous times.

They failed to arrive for their show in Keith so the first one they played was in Elgin, just days before 'Please Please Me' was released. The promoter, Albert Bonici, had been unsure whether people would know who they were so they were listed as 'the "Love Me Do" Boys' on the adverts, and his house band, the Alex Sutherland Quartet, were being relied on to lift the audience numbers. Just 80 people were there.

Albert deserves some credit for being a far-seeing promoter. He'd taken a big chance on the Beatles. But it says a lot for the band too that they fought their way through the weather and only missed one show.

The Two Red Shoes was known as the 'Tackety Beets' in the area, after farmers' boots with hobnails hammered in to extend their life. Bonici had had it built himself as an extension to his brother's café after a series of well-paying events in the local Drill Hall.

For Elgin to have a club was really unique. To have an actual club outside a city was very unusual – everything was municipal halls. At that time if you had an English band people would come just because they were English. Elgin was a very small town and people would come out of the woodwork from miles around. But the truth is it was a great club.

The Beatles' appearance certainly carved its name into history, but they also played three more shows on the following nights: Dingwall Town Hall, Bridge of Allan's Museum Hall, and Aberdeen's Beach Ballroom.

RODDIE HARPER: The Beatles had a couple of pints in the Commercial Bar in Dingwall and I remember thinking they were decent enough guys. I heard them later than night along with a few dozen others – I couldn't tell you how many there were although the Town Hall wasn't exactly crowded. I didn't think they were brilliant live but when 'Please Please Me' came out I thought it was a great record. Maybe they had an off-night! But it's always been said they signed a wall of the Commercial, and their autographs are still under the wooden panelling that was added later. That would be interesting.

BERT MacKAY: The Melotones were playing in the Strathpeffer Ballroom the night the Beatles played at Dingwall Town Hall. I saw them waiting on the steps for their gear to arrive. That night the show we played did well with over 1000 dancers in, but the Beatles' show was nearly empty so it closed early. They wound up coming to the Strath and a lot of my friends saw them, but I didn't.

MARY CRAWFORD: I got to the Town Hall after the Beatles had played. It usually stayed open until 1am but it was empty. The band were hanging about asking what they could do for the rest of the night and I suggested the Strath. I saw them there later that night and I thought the guitarist was very nice – I didn't know he would end up being George Harrison, of course! But I didn't get to dance with him.

COLIN McINTOSH: They didn't grab me in the Beach Ballroom. As far as I was concerned the Alex Harvey Soul Band could wipe the floor with them. I'll admit they had something with their own songs, and that was interesting because you didn't really get to play your own songs in those days. I never did get into the Beatles much – but the Stones were a different story when they came along.

Of course, it's not all about the number of people who saw or liked the Fab Four that January – it's about the storm that built up around them in the coming years and the changes it brought in its aftermath. Perhaps the old world of ballroom dancing could have kept jiving and rock'n'roll at bay – but the beat boom was to be so big it even took over the United States, something everyone in the British entertainment industry dreamed of.

Beatlemania: the Fab Four in a small Scottish club early in their career, above; the show which put the Two Red Shoes on the map, above right; autographs collected on the big night and the Elgin venue after its glory days, bottom right

THE ELGIN FOLK MUSIC CLUB
Presents

The "Love Me Do" Boys
THE BEATLES

plus

The Alex. Sutherland Sextet

in

THE TWO RED SHOES

on

THURSDAY, 3rd JANUARY

9 p.m. - 1 a.m.   Admission 6/-.

Buses return to Buckie, Forres,
Coast, Lossiemouth, etc.

Changing times: Edinburgh Beat Club, above, while McGoos and the International make their presence felt in the 1960s

McGOOS

18-20 HIGH STREET
EDINBURGH

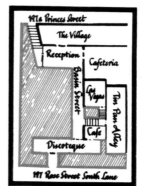

Albert Bonici did well out of it all too. It was common for promoters to insist on a return deal, where they had the right to re-book a band for a certain area in return for having taken the risk on the first booking. Bonici took advantage of the fact that Beatles manager Brian Epstein, like most of the businessmen in England, thought of Scotland as a wee backwater. Instead of getting an agreement to be the Beatles' exclusive agent for a region like the north of the country, Albert managed to cut a deal for the whole of Scotland. The Two Red Shoes and his other concern, the Ballerina Ballroom in Nairn, benefitted from that deal in the coming years – as did the dancers in the area too.

Great news for the young folk of the day – but for others it was a case of 'all good things ...'

BILL GRACIE: The beginning of the end for big bands had started in 1961. The whole scene changed and it wasn't long before dance halls started closing, just like a lot of the bands did.

I clearly remember being told by the management of the Hamilton Salon that a beat group would be playing the second half of one of our nights. And I don't remember any of us being in any way annoyed about it.

The night arrived, we played our half, then collected our instruments and headed up the stairs to the bandroom. As we went up, the group of young kids were making their way down, and one of them snarled at us: 'Make way for some real musicians!'

That did it for me. I turned a deaf ear to what was to become pop music and I didn't relax my attitude until I heard Ella Fitzgerald singing the Beatles' 'Can't Buy Me Love' some years later.

Although I can't say there were any hard feelings in general about the situation. It was just a progression of time. The Musicians' Union could do nothing because times were a-changin' and that was all there was to it.

Things happened quite slowly but I think for the public the big changes were you didn't have to buy a book full of dance steps, you didn't have to wear your Sunday best and you could just jump about like a demented dervish to pull the birds.

PETER KERR: The Clyde Valley Stompers had done very well. Peter and the Wolf had ended up with us doing a lot of telly – *Morecambe and Wise*, *Thank Your Lucky Stars*, *Cool for Cats* ... We did the title track for a Norman Wisdom film, *On the Beat*, and even appeared in Tommy Steele's movie, *It's All Happening*.

All through this the lineup was changing. Our agency did well in trying to replace Scots with Scots, but the time came when we wound up with this guy who just didn't fit – it wasn't anyone's fault, it just happens. But we replaced him with someone we chose ourselves, and that's when the agency took the hump.

They fired me as band leader, and when I went back and told the boys, they decided to leave with me.

The agency still owned the name and they got the Leathertown Jazz Band, an all-English band, back from Germany, dressed them in tartan and called them the Clyde Valley Stompers. They went out on the road – and lasted a week.

That was very sad – but everything was about to change anyway because of the Beatles. We'd all been thinking we were going to have to shift away from the trad stuff. But things were moving so fast that within a year there wasn't enough work for us to keep going, and that was the end of my career as a touring musician. No one could have seen all that coming. Not even the Beatles.

It wasn't a wipe-out right away – as long as people still wanted the more formal style of dancing, ballrooms were there to provide it. Regardless of the style of music you played,

Dance away the Blues at
"THE PALAIS"
to the Swinging Strict Tempo Tunes of
ANDY LOTHIAN'S ORCHESTRA
TUESDAY : 9 p.m. - Midnite, 4/-.
WEDNESDAY : CLUB NIGHT
8.45 p.m. - 12, 4/-; Members 3/-.
FRIDAY : 9.30 p.m. - 1 a.m., 6/6.
SATURDAY : 9 p.m. - 12, 6/-.
No Jiving No Teenagers
SUNDAY NITE —
TOP TEN — TEEN TIME at "The Palais"
7.30 - 10.30 p.m.

you could expect a fee of £25 per show, from which you had to pay your costs including transport, PA and so on. There was no rider although a lot of places provided tea and sandwiches.

You played a number of sets with breaks over a four-hour period, usually from 9pm until 1am or 10pm until 2am on Friday, but earlier on a Saturday. That was to allow everyone to get home and rested in time to attend the church of their choice on the Sabbath.

The paying public handed over three to five shillings for entry, which began to irritate bands who were playing to 500 dancers or more, knowing that £125 or more had been taken at the door while they were playing for less than a fifth of the cut. Groups began raising their fees, which added tension to the already tense balance between old and new guard.

Meanwhile, the licensing laws were still archaic. While down south many ballrooms had fully equipped bars which saw people drink the night away if they weren't dancing it away, in Scotland you still had to grab a drink in a pub before it shut at 9.30 or 10pm, ahead of your trip to the unlicenced dancin'. On Sundays you could only get a drink in a hotel, and only if you were a resident or a traveller – so you signed in using a false name, departure location and destination.

ALAN BROWN: The Kinema did have a wee bar but you were considered kind of a loser if you drank there. It just wasn't what you were there for. You weren't going to get a lassie if you were too drunk to dance with her. I remember one guy sitting pissed at a table with a lassie who was already getting bored with him. He threw up over the table and that was the end of his night. You really didn't want that happening to you.

PETE AGNEW: The Shadettes used to play Burntisland Palais every Saturday night. We had a knackered ex-gas-board van, painted bright yellow, and we wore bright yellow suits with a black 'S' embroidered on the pocket. To our eternal shame, now! When we finished we'd be too tired to change clothes, so we'd just pack up and head home. On the morning of 9 August 1963, just after we chugged up the hill out of Burntisland, we were pulled over by a police car. Two cops told us to get out of the van and unload it. We asked what the problem was, and they said there'd been a train robbery and a lot of money was involved. They said it had happened a couple of hours earlier, and we thought it must have been at Aberdour or Kirkcaldy or somewhere like that. But they said it was Buckinghamshire – four hundred miles away! And we're in a bright yellow van in bright yellow suits, mind you! We were probably the first, and definitely the most colourful, suspects in the Great Train Robbery ...

BRIAN NOBILE: The Browns eventually got the St Margaret's Hall lease back from the Kinema management – but the venue was gutted by fire only a few weeks afterwards, during Ballroom Enterprises' final booking, which was a boxing match. The thing about that last night was that some of the boxers were also bouncers at the Kinema. So that led to the theory they'd set fire to the hall – but nobody could prove anything. It did leave the Kinema with the whole dance thing to themselves and they made a fortune, especially after they extended the ballroom in 1964.

The Shadettes in 'train robber' outfits

Incidentally, it's true Cecil Hunter turned down the Beatles for the Kinema in 1963. He was offered the band on their first tour of the year, before they got really big, but thought they were a bit pricey. By the time Cecil was offered them again they were too big for the KB before its extension was built – and that's why the Beatles played an all-seated gig at the Rio in Kirkcaldy instead.

WILLIE KEITH: I'd been going to the dancin' in the Railway Hall, Inverurie, for a couple of months. I was starting to get quite confident with the girls and I'd had my eye on this wee brunette for a couple of weeks – only every time I nearly plucked up the courage to make a move someone else was there first. But it was quiet this night and I really fancied my chances. Just as I sorted out what thing to say in my head, the music stopped and the hall manager announced: 'Is there a William Keith in the room? His mother wants to speak to him at the door!' Talk about rid-faced! It took me months to get the courage to go back to the Railway Hall. And all my mother wanted was to tell me she'd be home late that night from her work. It ended well, though – not only did I get to dance with the wee brunette eventually, I married her six years later. Sadly she remembers that night all too well, so there's no point me trying to forget it ...

ALAN SMITH: My dad had an absolute belter of a chat-up line which he used in the Dennistoun Palais. He'd go up to a girl and say: 'Stick with me, hen, and I'll show you the world.' One night the girl replied: 'Aye, right ...' but my dad pulled out a pocket atlas! It got him the dance and 47 years on they're still together. Do I take after my dad? I hope so ...

7 Shoulder to shoulder, back and forth – like exotic birds mating

IT'S FAIR to say the people who'd gained most from the post-war dancin' boom fought hard to keep rock'n'roll in the gutter, where they believed it belonged.

The fact was that a lot of musicians who'd spent their lives in the industry just didn't like the idea of young folk coming in who couldn't read music and hadn't served their time. But the counter-fact was that more and more people were getting into what the young folk played.

Still, the powers that be held on. They'd banned jiving in a lot of places, and some others had even banned teenagers from getting in. They tried to ban beat groups as well – but that wasn't going to be so simple.

RONNIE SIMPSON: Ballroom owners in west-central Scotland came to an agreement with the Musicians' Union that a band had to have at least seven members. Most combos at that time were four or five strong, and maybe the odd six, but nobody had seven. So we were all out in the cold.

But the powers didn't have control over *all* the halls – they ran the 'biggest most popular' ones just because they were the only option for the dancing public. So we started booking community centres and ran Friday night hops against the formal dance nights.

The established dance halls didn't want to change their 'proper' status on those nights. Still, demand for our music was high and we were denting the ballrooms' income, so the Palais venues started beat nights on Mondays and Wednesdays and the ballrooms did Tuesday, Thursdays and Sundays, and things like that.

ARCHIE YOUNG: The Cavendish in Edinburgh came to its own compromise. Monday night was for the younger ones dancing to the local pop group while Wednesday was ballroom dancing for the older members of the public. On

Friday and Saturday the Cavendish Dance Band played downstairs and the pop group played in the smaller hall on the top floor.

HARRY ANDERSON: I always think one night in the Coldstream Town Hall says a lot about how things were changing. The younger people in the area were excited because it was the first night a rock'n'roll group were to play at the interval for one of the usual jazz bands. The hall had always said they'd never let rock'n'roll in, but they'd had to go back on it. Still, tensions were a bit high.

I wish I could remember the name of the group who played but I was never really all that into the groups themselves – it was the music and the dancing for me. Whoever they were, they were dressed up as cowboys from the movies and the singer had a big long bullwhip. The time came for them to play and the older folk moved to the side of the hall and sat down. Not that they were angry or anything, but they wanted to see how it would go.

The group started up playing – and the noise was amazing. It's nothing by today's standards but we'd never heard it for real and it blew us away, and so we were all up jiving away for all we were worth. The singer was cracking his whip like a madman as he sang and it was really brilliant.

But it was all too much for the hall manager, who used to kick people out for jiving. He marched onto the stage and waved his hands until the group stopped playing. We all stopped as well and watched as he told the band to turn it right down or they wouldn't get paid. They didn't have much choice – they turned it down. But after a couple of minutes it was back to full volume.

This time the manager came up from the back of the hall with the three bouncers and you could tell there was going to be trouble. Everyone stopped dancing until there was only the group playing and the manager and stewards in front of him. I don't know if the singer had seen what was going on, he was so wrapped up in his performance – but he tried to crack his whip in the air and it caught on the wee mirrorball on the ceiling, and it came crashing down and landed at the manager's feet.

There must have been about ten seconds of silence but it felt like hours. The manager looked at the smashed mirrorball then at the singer, and the singer looked back at him. Then the manager just walked off the floor, leaving the bouncers standing there looking stupid. After a few moments the band started playing again and it was almost like it have never happened. I often wonder if the manager retired that night – I certainly never saw him again.

RONNIE SIMPSON: We found ourselves playing more or less seven days a week. For us it was the Airdrie Palais or the Trocadero in Hamilton on Mondays. Then the Flamingo in Cardonald on Tuesdays or Thursdays. On Wednesdays we'd

The System's big night in a deceptively small-looking Flamingo Ballroom, above, came after a career in smaller venues, right, and local youth clubs, below. Singer Martin Griffiths fronted Beggars Opera before becoming a disco star in Germany

either do Bobby Jones' in Ayr or go back to the Trocadero. Two weekends a month we were on the road, working for Albert Bonici in the Highlands or for Bert 'Bapper' Ewan in Aberdeenshire. Those weekends were great because it took us out of the central-belt rat race and also the money was four or five times better.

We had to change our name too – ballrooms didn't like 'the Midlanders Combo' because it sounded too miners' welfare, or it was too rough, or sounded too out-of-town for their audiences. The people at the Flamingo suggested Sol Byron and the Impacts. Hey – for two gigs a week they could call us anything they liked!

The floodgates were opening, and actually the new music did behave a bit like water, finding a natural path towards the mainstream. It was new, it was exciting, and it was soon going to be everywhere – not just in the places the powers that be wanted to keep it.

Every youth club in the country was bouncing to the Beatles and all the acts who'd come afterwards. Most clubs had their own bands, and in many cases more than one. There just seemed to be no stopping it.

MARTIN GRIFFITHS: Our beat group, the System, were resident band in the Stamperland Institute in Netherlee, where the dance was a sort of shoulder-to-shoulder backwards and forwards movement – not unlike the mating dance of some exotic birds in the wild. We never had the chance to dance because we were the dance makers and expected our girl, if we had one, to be very loyal. But there's not much you could do if you were on stage and she disappeared with one of the roadies!

Girls danced with girls either in pairs or in a circle and always with their handbag in front of them on the dance floor. The boys hung around trying to pluck up enough courage to ask the question or just watched the group.

The Institute was always packed and we arrived just before opening time with all our amplifiers and the drums in Ricky Gardiner's little Austin A30. Unloading and sound check didn't take long – we had no lights, smoke effects or PA. It was just plug in and play.

It's easy to form the idea that there was some kind of line drawn, where the younger musicians elbowed in and the older musicians wandered off into the sunset. But that's not the case. Many people embraced the new music as another turn of the wheel of life. Many found they enjoyed it, even thought it was different from the more formal styles of the past. Although many found they also had to live through some of their long-valued myths of the music scene being burst like bubbles ...

FRANK FERRI: Little did I know when I became a regular at the Palais de Dance

I'd be performing on its revolving stage a dozen years later ... My band, the Jokers, had been booked as the support band for the Tam Paton Showband. Not many people know but he was an excellent keyboard player and ran the Crusaders featuring Tam White, Toto McNaughton and Frankie Connor before he did the Bay City Rollers.

My time came on stage at the Palais. I'd always wondered what was involved in moving that massive revolving stage when it was time for the second band to come burling round. Surprise, surprise, there was no electronic wizardry – it was just a manually-operated wheel like the mangle your granny would use to squeeze water from her washing. Another little bit of showbiz magic dissolved!

DEREK BROWN: My dad, Eddie 'Edo' Brown, played bass in all the dance halls in Glasgow during the 60s and 70s with Dave Mason, George Patterson and others. He remembers a night at the Dennistoun Palais where the saxophonist sitting beside him was drunk but on his final warning from the bandleader. The stage started to revolve for them and the saxophonist threw up into his horn – and had to pretend to play for the rest of the show. As you can imagine, that was an experience for my dad.

ROBERT KELLY: My dad worked in the Denny Palais and he used to say the revolving stage was a weapon instead of a piece of machinery. Rival bands would get their friends to wind the wheel too fast, trying to put the other band off. He told me one night there were four guys turning it for the Joe Loss Band, instead of the usual one or two, and it came round so fast the wheels came off the rail. The Joe Loss Band had to keep playing while sitting at a steep angle ...

When I played there with the Blue Beats I watched the other band like a hawk to make sure they kept their hands off the wheel. I was so busy looking round the whole time that I didn't notice the best-looking girl in the room was watching me all night. By the time the rest of the band told me she was away with someone else – and of course when the stage revolved it all went normally. It did feel a bit weird though.

BRIAN YOUNG: The revolving stage at the Locarno had to be watched. Your guitar case could get smashed if you didn't move it out the way in time. I've seen it happen during the gang warfare. I've also seen the bodies carried off the dance floor over the dancers' heads ...

FRANK FERRI: In 1964 my band, the Jokers, split up – some thought we were better than we were and wanted to go full-time, but I knew we'd never been that good. I'd only got into it because my brother needed help filling the band – at 27 and with two kids I thought I was too old for it anyway. But we'd had a great trip to look back on. Normally we'd been paid £10 or £12, on occasion £15, which wasn't very good. But the Yanks at Kirknewton always paid better and you even got a meal, usually a burger and fries. They'd booked us for Christmas Eve at £50, which was a king's ransom – but unknown to us it was the officers' dance, in dress uniforms ... After a new number we realised we weren't going down too well. The sergeant who booked us came to the rescue by suggesting a combined do with the sergeants' mess – which solved the problem because Lulu and the Luvvers were covering that gig.

We'd supported Acker Bilk in the Haddington Corn Exchange. Sadly only about 50 people showed up, so we had a few drinks and a jam session with Acker and his band. We'd supported Dave Dee, Dozy, Beaky, Mick and Titch in Selkirk, where we opened with their current hit 'Hold Tight' and got away with it, no problems. We'd been in the middle of a riot during our last number at Portobello Town Hall, and ironically it had been the Animals' 'We Gotta Get Out of This Place'. We'd been the first band to play Leith Pageant on the back of a flatbed truck – someone lent us a generator, we adjusted the ampage of our gear and away we went, playing on the move. Great stuff!

Albert Bonici remained at the front of developments. He managed Johnny and the Copycats, and boasted of their top-quality tour van which included a record player, tape player, radio, reclining seats and wardrobes for their outfits. He set up the country's first independent record label, Norco, to release Copycats singles. Andy Lothian had ALP Records in Dundee, Waverley Records was in Edinburgh and there was even a short-lived Flamingo Records based out of the west-coast ballroom.

CATH McDONALD: The Flamingo used to be an old cinema and they still had the balcony although the seats were obviously taken out. The Singleton brothers ran it. At first they had a big band with a pop group on at the interval but it was soon seen that they were more popular. So the big band moved out and Sol Byron became the main band, and the Poets became the interval band. As is the way, the Poets became the most popular group.

RONNIE SIMPSON: The Poets were given a guest spot at our regular busy Tuesday night at the Flamingo. We did not get the impression that they'd played a date before and, frankly, we thought they were terrible. So we were really pissed off when we discovered that the ballroom owners had invited Rolling Stones manager Andrew Loog Oldham up to see them.

I think the Flamingo people were quite taken aback at our reaction. Sol Byron and the Impacts were pulling in hundreds of dancers two nights a week, two nights which had been dead before we came in – and then they set up an audition with Loog Oldham for these kids?

As compensation they got us booked into Bryce Laing's Craighall Studio in Edinburgh to record our own single on Flamingo Records. We recorded Marvin Gaye's 'Pride And Joy' plus a B-side, John D Loudermilk's 'I Shall Not Steal'.

Of course, neither we nor the Flamingo people knew what to do with the record, so nothing ever happened with it. You could buy it at the Flamingo but that was it. I see it on eBay for £50 sometimes these days ...

We were still a force to be reckoned with, so the next time a major label was auditioning we were invited up the three or four flights of stairs to the Lindella Club. It was a two-horse race: us versus the Gleneagles, who featured a wee Lindella jiver who sang a bit. The end result was they changed their name to Lulu and the Luvvers, and we lost out again.

Sol Byron took this as a bit of a sign and left the band to join a supergroup made up of the best of the guys from the first wave of beat groups: Sol Byron and the Senate.

CATH McDONALD: The dress sense was terrible for us punters. The girls wore straight checked skirts down past your knees with one pleat in the back and crew neck jumpers. I must have looked like my granny. The guys wore suits with short jackets and straight tight trousers.

DAVE VALENTINE: We rehearsed just round the corner from Edinburgh's Abano Club in our guitarist's dad's pub – right beside the ladies' toilets, which were often left open to the wind. Ladies of the night did not give a jot as they sat in there, drawers at their feet, shouting at us as we trooped in to rehearse.

The Abano wasn't doing too well. Bands like the Blues Brotherhood used to play to a handful of people. We decided to go round and meet the owner, a weird grey-haired man with an equally weird wife, and asked to play what would end up as the Hipple People's first resident gig.

It soon built up until we had 200 people queuing round the corner – I think the fact we were still at high school helped. We were on a cut of the gate and it did quite well. I'm not sure how long it lasted but I remember one night when the owner came up, a bit sad, to tell us the crowd was down – then produced even more money for us than he had the previous week. I'll also never forget the smell of dogshit in the metal lift we had to use to get the gear upstairs.

There was a shared band room in the Place and you never knew who you'd run into there. Glasgow and Edinburgh bands had a really good cameraderie backstage, though. One night I was greeted with the vision of the tall one from Unit Four Plus Two peeing in the sink as if it was an everyday thing to do. Another time I saw Edinburgh bassist Scott Murray dancing a rhumba bollock-naked with a piece of ribbon tied round his winkle, much to the enjoyment of a Glasgow band in the room. The fun we had!

REG REID: The Gamp and Bungy's were good places to go, but my formative days at the dancin' were spent at the Place all weekend, sleeping all day Saturday and Sunday. Sunday night was the best – always the same faces and quality bands playing like the Boston Dexters and the Blues Council. Big Wally was always ready to forego his door duties and join the band on stage with his bongo drums.

One time Lonnie Donegan played. He was excellent, but I was with some lass who was more interested in the fact that the pop singer Craig Douglas was in the audience. She grabbed my Place membership card to get his autograph. The following week I was in the Palais and the Animals turned up after playing the Usher Hall. Long John Baldry joined them in the back café and it was my turn to be awestruck. All I had was my Place card, so the Animals signed the front then Eric Burdon handed it to Baldry, who turned it over looking for a place to sign, and found Craig Douglas' scrawl. Did they take the piss out of me!

BRIAN HOGG: A lot of the Glasgow bands would play where I was staying, Galston in the west of Edinburgh, then move on to a venue closer to the city centre, and finish up at an all-nighter – so they'd be doing three gigs in the one night. There was a difference between the east and west coast bands ... Edinburgh bands would do an obscure Kinks track but the Glasgow bands would do an obscure soul track. They were less kinda 'poppy' if you like.

Aberdeen's Beach Ballroom found its way to retaining its position as an institution. It was built to service ballroom dancers, and it was run by Adam Sharp who ultimately came down to manage the Plaza and died there in his 70s, still a manager. It's rumoured he lived in the Plaza and he nearly did, but he actually lived just round the corner.

At the Beach he taught people ballroom dancing. When the beat bands came in he started booking us in. The Weavles, the Poets and several others were very popular there.

Frank Ferri's stage life, including meeting
Johnny Kidd, top right, and Acker Bilk,
middle right, plus gigs in the Place, top left,
the Cephas Club, middle left, and on a
flatbed truck in Leith, left

The cattle-market vibe rendered itself in the Beach like so: everyone went round the hall anti-clockwise to get a good look at the talent before pouncing. It made troublemakers easy to spot – they were the ones trying to go clockwise. If you didn't meet your fellow 'Beach Babies' under the clock after the dancin' it meant you'd pulled.

The paying public had never been so spoilt for choice. No matter what you wanted you could find it most nights of the week. The beat groups were getting a fairer share of the game and the older band were still being given their place – it was an uneasy truce.

Although perhaps 'truce' is completely the wrong word ...

MARTIN GRIFFITHS: Even in the youth clubs, violence was never far away. The safest place to be was often on stage, hanging on to our amps while all hell broke loose in the hall. Some girls smuggled in sharpened metal combs to give to their boyfriends inside who were on the lookout for trouble.

FRANK FERRI: I was a steward in the Gamp club for about a year. We had our moments but there wasn't much trouble. There were six of us, headed by a guy named Stewart Togher, who was a hard-man bodybuilder, and three of his mates. Me and my mate Peter McTeague, a workmate from Ferranti, were more or less pinned on with not a lot to do. For a wee while a bunch of hard nuts from Glasgow came over to test the team out, but it didn't amount to much.

ARCHIE YOUNG: At the Cavendish we wore maroon blazers with the initials 'CD' on the breast pocket. You worked two nights a week of your choice and had to work Friday and Saturday, and you got home on a late bus put on by the Cavendish for free as long as you provided protection for the driver. For all that we were paid a mere £5 a week.

Many of the patrons became good friends. Most of them were out to have a good time, get a date and go home. I enjoyed meeting the public and talking and laughing with them.

The job was really all about diplomacy – except during the Glasgow fortnight. One night we were told the Tongs were coming through to cause trouble. Sure enough they did. They were armed with razors, bayonets, hunting knives and butcher's knives. The fighting started inside the Cavendish but we managed to get them outside and hammered them until they were arrested. I don't know if they really were the Tongs but they were shouting: 'Up the Tongs'.

Once a lad was thrown out when I was looking after the queue outside. He tried to get back in so I put him out again. As I threw him off the premises a man stepped forward and shouted, 'Hey you!' He was coming up quite fast and he put his hand in his coat. I thought he was going for a knife so I slugged him on the chin and he went down. It turned out he was a plain-clothes policeman going for his warrant card – but I wasn't charged because he'd been in the wrong.

PETE AGNEW: In Cumnock and places like that they'd say, 'When the fight starts ...' Not 'If a fight starts' but '*When* the fight starts'! They'd tell us: 'When the fight starts you just keep playing.' You were basically supplying the soundtrack to a war.

Here in Fife they used to say trouble came on the Glasgow buses. They weren't necessarily Glasgow buses, but they were from the west. It was a recipe for bother because of the mix. We were the resident band in the Burntisland Palais, and it was really falling to bits. When it rained the roof would leak and they'd put buckets on the dance floor. People would dance round these eight buckets. But when 'the fight' started, that was eight weapons sitting there ready!

When the buses would come through they'd never be told, 'You're not getting in', because the dance halls just wanted to make money. If they punched each other about for a while who cared? They'd be back next week anyway. And I think a lot of them just came for the rumble anyway.

A boy used to sit on the roof of the resident stage in the Kinema where we played when the guest band came in. I can't mind his name but he was a wee baldy guy and he just sat up there. He just watched the crowd and if someone started up he just pointed the spotlight at him and the bouncers moved in – it worked. Everything was nipped in the bud.

IAN MOFFATT: Growing up in Prestwick like we did, you were always up against it with the Yanks from the air base. If you wanted to stand a chance of a lumber you had to learn a bit of swagger from an early age.

We thought we'd nailed it when we formed a group with this older guy, George. He had a decent guitar and a great voice, and a song called 'America' which he sang like 'America-ha-ha!' and that was exactly the kind of attitude we wanted. I mean, you'd have broken your mate's arm to go to the USA but you weren't going to admit that ... We even called the band the Home Rockers. Get it?

George reckoned he could get any lassie he wanted just by staring at her. It worked a lot of the time – he'd lean against the counter at the coffee bar and pick a victim, and eventually she'd come over, all shy-like, and he'd ask her out – like she was going to say no after all that! I learned the trick that if he picked a lassie I liked the look of, I'd go up to her and say, 'He doesn't mean it, hen, he's blind ...'

We started taking after George and getting a bit too clever for our own boots. We hadn't done all that many gigs and the ones we had done weren't exactly what you'd call memorable. Or if they were it wasn't for the right reasons.

One night I went straight up to a lassie in Bobby Jones' even though she was in with a guy from the air base. I waited till he'd gone off somewhere, of course. She'd just taken her hair down so I said: 'Alright, hen, is anything else coming

Stars of the Strath: Johnny Law and the MI5, above, and Johnny Little and the Giants, below

down?' That moment her boyfriend turned up and thumped me – I clattered to the floor but at least I had the presence of mind to say, 'Oh right, me!'

But it all came to an end the night George was chatting up a lassie after we'd done an interval slot with the main band. He was leaning there all smart-ass like, with her mates all around them, and she told him: 'You've got a great voice – it's a pity you use it to talk shite!' I actually saw him crumple as all the lassies fell about laughing at him.

I went over to cheer him up and said, 'Never mind, George, remember the attitude in the song, "America-ha-ha" — we don't need these Yank followers!' But George said, 'What do you mean?' Turns out he wasn't singing 'America-ha-ha', he was just singing 'America' with a funny twang, and the song was about how he wanted to live there.

That was the end of our band – but I hear George made it to Canada, if not the States.

JOAN DUNCAN: I was allowed to go to the Majestic in Glasgow because a good crowd went there. I certainly wasn't allowed to go to the Barrowlands.

When we went to the pictures my boyfriend Bobby, who became my husband, would get me home around twenty past ten. We'd stand on the landing having a wee cuddle and my dad would rattle the front door from the inside, saying, 'You'll get the subway if you go now, son!' Ten minutes later he'd be saying, 'You'll get the subway if you run, son!' Then at eleven o'clock he'd come out on the landing in his pyjamas, carrying his alarm clock and saying, 'Right, off you go and walk home!'

Then I'd go inside and start taking off my outfit – false eyelashes, hairpiece, makeup, the lot. My dad would say, 'You look like a refugee from a Chinese ballet company! Get that stuff off your face!'

And he warned me: 'There's not a bit of you that's real ... that boy's going to get the shock of his life if he ever gets you!'

8 The ballroom was electrifying ... the smell of excitement

THIS was the world I entered when I decided to become E Tobin Enterprises and manage a group of my schoolfriends. It made a lot of sense: they wanted to play music, I wanted to make money, and we all wanted to meet girls. We called ourselves the Bo Weavles: George Gilmour on vocals, Ricky Archibald on bass, Jimmy Brand on drums, Dave Batchelor on keyboards and Zal Cleminson on guitar. Of course, Zal was to become the legendary guitarist with the Sensational Alex Harvey Band and Dave kept working with us throughout most of those years. But we didn't know any of that then – all we knew is that we were 'Scotland's first boy band'.

I don't even know what I was doing there. I probably broke into Davie's house and when they came in I pretended I was early for the band meeting. I could never play a note ... so I couldn't do anything else useful but get into management. The thing is, if you were in a band you were magical to girls, and the aura extended round those who were with the band. I got as close as I could: 'Are you in the band?' 'Nearly – I'm in the van. That's good enough, isn't it?'

DAVE BATCHELOR: I was training to be a civil engineer and Eddie was a shipping clerk but the rest of the band were at school. Zal lived next door to me and he and George were doing the acoustic guitar thing, without any real idea of forming a band. I got a guitar too and it happened about then – I remember being in our front room with cheap electric guitars, messing about. Suddenly we were a band.

We started playing about with Beatles numbers and stuff from the 50s. One afternoon we were out the back of our house, doing 'Only You', the Platters song, and we had a guy who was meant to be the first drummer. He didn't have a drum – he had a bike wheel and a stick, and he spun the wheel then pressed the stick into it to make a rhythm sound. Everyone was looking at him, thinking: 'I don't know if you're going to make it to the final lineup, mate ...'

So our first drummer was sacked without even having a drum! Jimmy Brand had one, at least – it was a marching drum, the Partick True Defenders or something like that. We told him we weren't going to be a marching band – we were planning to stay still.

Our first gig was in a local hall in Pennilee. At the start everyone does everything for nothing, so we played for a youth club. They actually weren't that bad – people stayed and some people liked it. We gravitated to Paisley Town Hall, and Zal had a broken leg at the time. He played the gig with a big plaster on – in those days there was no talk of not doing the gig. But Paisley wasn't local, so that was a big move. It was almost like going abroad.

DAVE BATCHELOR: Zal could spin about on his plastered leg because he had a big heel on it. It looked great!

Every Saturday we'd go into a wee record shop in Langside where the guy got in all the latest soul and R&B records from the States. So we weren't playing chart stuff, but we were playing stuff with a great groove which was coming from the States. We were playing stuff the kids didn't know, but it had great rhythm so they could dance to it. You'd never think about writing stuff in those days – you concentrated on learning to play this stuff very well.

The big step up was playing in the town. We played the Picasso Club, and to play there and not be booed off you had to be okay. That's where all the bands hung out, so when we got a residency there on a Wednesday that was us on the circuit with all the bands.

RONNIE SIMPSON: Johnny Wilson moved from Glasgow to London where, I believe, he did quite well. But don't ask me as what. Bert Ewen was always dedicated to ballroom dancing but tolerated this new music and moved with the changes.

Duncan McKinnon was a real character. The fun part was phoning him with a few acts to sell. As we talked, he'd be tearing through a bottle of 'something' – and as the call wore on he changed from discussing the details of business to ranting about how 'young bastards like you are killing the business demanding fees for bands that aren't worth a fuck.' I learned that if I was speaking to Duncan then I should have a refreshment at hand too.

The Fehilly brothers were a bit loose cannon. Bands would travel to the Strathpeffer Ballroom, one of their regular gigs, to find the other brother was holding the cash somewhere like Alloa. The following week when the band appeared in Alloa, the money was waiting for them in Strathpeffer with the other brother.

The rapidly-growing scene needed a dedicated agent to get the better bands into the better gigs, because dance organisers were used to having one resident band and didn't know the good from the bad. But who had their finger on the pulse? Who was in constant contact with those promoters? Who'd just got his jotters from the steel-work? Yes – t'was I! So Music & Cabaret Entertainments was born at 150 Hope Street.

I found out there were agents outside of Glasgow and began making contact. The band were soon playing everywhere, from Wick to Carlisle, Stranraer to Eyemouth. We were doing six nights a week and three gigs on a Saturday – that's how much dancing there was. It was astounding. And of course it was a great help to be working with Ronnie Simpson's agency.

DAVE BATCHELOR: We had to learn six or seven Jim Reeves songs before we played the Strathpeffer Spa for the first time. They were like, 'Do ye ken "Please Stay"? Aye? Well, you'd better or you're no' leavin' the hall ...'

BERT MacKAY: The Melotones played at the Strath more than any other group, and I even met my wife there, of course! One night I remember a grey-haired old lady offering me ten pounds to play 'Wheels', because it had been her late husband's favourite tune. I played it a few times for her that night.

ARCHIE YOUNG: At the Cavendish, like a lot of dance halls, the women paid less than the men to get in. But in return for that they weren't allowed to to refuse any man a dance. If they did, they were given their money back and told to leave. That changed when the women argued they shouldn't have to dance with someone they didn't like, and after that everyone paid the same five shillings to get in.

At that time *everyone* was participating in the dancin'. Ballrooms were still busy, clubs were busy, town halls were busy – there weren't many age restrictions so everyone was part of it. In Stranraer the Weavles played to an audience ranging from teenagers to grandparents – mainly because the venue held bingo games before the bands played.

We played in Portpatrick Town Hall to a full house of 300 people. The band finished the show, went into the dressing room, cleaned themselves up and went out to see who there was to dance with – the answer was no one. They'd all gone. They must have got into a spaceship because there's nowhere to go in Portpatrick. We never went back.

At St Patrick's Hall in Coatbridge you had to stop halfway through the set so the priest could come on and say a prayer. He'd say his prayer, everyone would pray along, then you'd do the next song.

In the Auchinleck Community Centre, Zal fell off the stage – and kept playing. I saw him disappear but I could still hear the guitar. I was filled with admiration for him. What a soldier. We played at the Lido in Balloch with Billy Fury and Billy was amazing. He dropped a handkerchief on stage and bent over backwards to pick it up – all the girls were screaming.

I saw an incredible fight in Mintlaw Station by Peterhead. But the interesting thing about fights up north is that they'd never kick you while you were down. You could wind up rolling about on the floor with someone but once you were down you didn't have people raining kicks and punches down on you, which you got in Glasgow. The bouncers managed to take this fight outside where it continued for a while. Then everyone who'd been fighting, covered in blood and everything, decided to go back into the dancin'. The hall manager held his hand up to them and said: 'No, no, no – you'll have to pay!' He took another ten bob off them all and they went back in for a dance.

BRIAN NOBILE: My favourite memories of the Kinema was when I became a DJ and singer. I was lead vocalist in my school band, the Diplomats, when the Red Hawks were looking for a replacement for Alan Jordan. Cecil Hunter invited me to audition. I went along on a beautiful Sunday afternoon and sang 'Wild Thing', 'Can't Buy Me Love' and 'You Make Me Feel So Young'. I didn't get the job – but the memory of playing with my idols the Red Hawks will remain with me for ever. I was note-perfect, by the way ... Later I became DJ at the Sound 70 when it opened as Dunfermline's first disco.

CATH McDONALD: I used to work in the Barrowlands around 1965. When you look at the place now you would never believe how plush the ladies' cloakrooms were then. They had pink leather seats and couches and highly polished mirrors all around. The bouncers wore blue uniforms in summer and maroon in winter and only the top brass wore dinner suits. The Locarno's cloakroom wasn't as plush – it was much more tack. Their colours were red and gold and the seats were material, and they were bolted to the floor.

DONNIE MacIVER: The caretaker in the Dingwall Town Hall was a right wee character. Dot was his name and he was obsessed with selling wee bottles of lemonade to everyone. He'd keep the windows closed till the place was too hot, but when he was asked to open them he'd say, 'Not till the lemonade's all been sold!'

DONALD PIRIE: We'd played our set at a certain hall in Aberdeen on a Friday night, and we were heading off for a drink in my mate's hotel. When we got there he told us an old friend had called for us and we were to call back no matter what time it was. Turned out a well-to-do businessman in the area was looking for a band to play a private show later on that very night, and the money was excellent.

We went back to the hall to collect our gear – but it was locked up and the hallkeeper was away home, and no one knew where he lived. So we broke in

Meet the Bo Weavles: the band in their stolen curtain outfits, main pic; on the cover of their own magazine, right, and in a promo poster, below

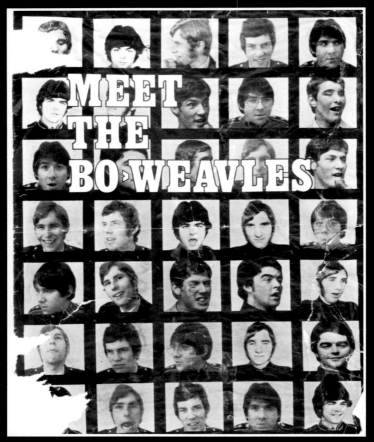

Zal Cleminson prepares to meet the girls after a Bo Weavles show, promoted by cards like the one below

The
BO.
WEAVLES

Sole Management: E.TOBIN
    96 Bowfield Crescent,
    Glasgow, S.W.2.
    Tel: MOS 7552.

            F A N   C L U B S

GLASGOW   RGT. PARK
    36   ne Place,
        Murray,
        East Kilbride.

FIFE and N. SCOTLAND
            PAT ALLISON
        78 Denwalk,
        Methil, Fife.

            Photographed by R. ANDERSON.

through a wee store room at the back, got the gear, got the gig and got paid. When we went back to the hall on the Saturday we were told there'd been a break-in and all our gear had gone. We made a lot of racket about having to borrow guitars and drums at the last minute on a Saturday night but somehow we muddled through – and the insurance company paid up on the claim too!

The Weavles played the Co-op Hall in Rosyth. We went down very badly, and that's why it's bad luck for us that the Co-op Hall was the collection point for all the milk bottles in Dunfermline. We didn't have the van that night – we had a bus for some reason, and the crowd launched cases and cases of bottles. It was like a wall of crates coming in. Derek Nicol was there with a big steward but he couldn't save us because there were too many of them. We just had to run.

We went to the Blantyre Celtic Club with an Orange amp – it was just an amplifier. Orange stuff was good because it was very robust, and I'd send bands out all the time with it. I didn't think about it, but of course they don't like that sort of thing in places like Blantyre. A girl called Little Egypt saved us – she was a member of the women's section of the Carlton Tongs, and as we tried to make our escape she smashed a bottle and claimed the entire population of Blantyre, it seemed, for a fight. No one dared to take her up on it.

KATE BLACKBURN: Every weekend was like a ritual when I was a teenager. You tried your best to get a new outfit for Friday night and went to work with your hair in rollers – or left your hairpiece at home in rollers. You rushed home from work and were out the door for the bus by 7.30 at the latest, made up to the nines.

You started off maybe having a Carlsberg Special – it was five and six but it was the quickest way to get merry, then it was on to a club until the early hours. You had to walk home because the buses had stopped and very few people had access to a car.

On the Saturday morning you'd get up, recover and start all over again for that night. Sunday was spent trying to catch up on your sleep, then on Monday it was back to work, saving up for Friday again. In between times you caught up with your pals to see how they'd got on, who'd bagged off with whom and how they compared. Great times!

Fashion started off with mini skirts then moved on to tent dresses. We tried to keep up with the top fashion of the week, but we were always smart.

ROBERT LOW: Could have been the Locarno or the Barrowland or even F&F's – but I was 16 and even if it was pelting it down, I didn't care for I was off to get a lumber and listen to Geno Washington and the Ram Jam Band. Their album *Hand Clappin' Foot Stompin' Funky Butt Live* was out and the track everyone wanted to get dancin' to was 'Hold on, I'm Comin'' – a blaster.

I was in a sharp suit, drainpipe trousers and a brand-new pair of chisel-toed, elastic-sided boots in dark purple. I was ecstatic about the footwear because my mother was anal about shoes and had always bought mine for me from when I was old enough to wear them. They were always from Clarks and always sensible. These chisel toes would have had her tearing her hair out, which was why I'd bought them with my own money – and also why they were so cheap.

I walk to the venue in the pouring rain, queue, pay the last of my money and get in. The place is packed and the heat from hundreds of dancing bodies is making steam, but I don't care – I am lumbered and showing my moves to the beehive hairdo of my choice.

Then I see my shoes. Cheap leather, soaked and steam-dried, they're curling at the ends like a pair of square-toed Turkish slippers. I look like Aladdin's twat cousin and, worse, the soles are parting from the uppers.

Cue exit. Cue walk home in the wet in my socks. But Geno was great.

DAVE VALENTINE: The Top Storey Club in Edinburgh was also near the Hipple People's rehearsal room. I remember an early version of the Bay City Rollers called the Motown Stompers, who supported us one night and didn't do too well – in fact they were booed off. That was embarrassing for me because Nobby, their lead singer, was going out with my sister at the time.

I remember seeing the Pretty Things, who were very loose and bluesy before they turned into 10cc. It was mighty to behold Phil May singing while he took slugs from a bottle of whisky. At the other end of the scale was Billy J Kramer, who was obviously shitting himself before he played. Long before I was in a band I used to try to copy his singing voice, using a saucepan to mimic the echo effect, saddo that I am! Most of the city's top bands of the time played there – the Beachcombers, the Moonrakers, who were Edinburgh's Kinks, the Embers and Three's A Crowd.

Those days were wild if you were young men like us. Albert Bonici booked us for the famous Two Red Shoes, so we played where the 'biggest band in the world, ever' played (see page 66). Sadly it didn't last much longer, although Albert still had other interests, including the Ballerina in Nairn. Albert was an agent through and through. To illustrate his character, he was charged with smuggling watches into the UK by wearing them all the way up his arms. He was a genuine wide-boy – all credit to him, but it was luck. It could have been anyone, but it was him, bless him.

Auchterarder Town Hall was a great place. It had a capacity of three or four hundred and it was always full. It was always a great town for dancing. The steward was Andy Robin, the wrestler, who owned Hercules the Bear. Andy stewarded the whole place himself. Such was his fame that no one ever caused any trouble unless they were mad. If they did, he'd go through the room like the Tasmanian Devil – the crowd would part and he'd throw people up in the air. That seemed to be his trick. Andy lived in a caravan out the back. His message for troublemakers was: 'If you want to make something of it, that's where I'll be.' I don't think anyone ever chapped his door.

The Strathpeffer Pavilion, still overseen at that time by the Fehilly brothers, remained a force to be reckoned with in the north of the country. It was certainly playing host to all the big names, and was even accepting the fact that it could make things easier for bands to play there by allowing the further-travelled ones to stay the night. They made top-floor rooms available – but because the building was alarmed, and almost certainly also because the building had drink stored in it, the bands who stayed there had to be locked in at night.

The trick was to park your van near the eaves of the roof, so that anyone who'd managed to find a reason to be back late could carefully climb up and get in the window. Only a few are known to have fallen during the brave climb, and if anyone was seriously injured they had the sense to hide it from the Strath's management.

ARTHUR SCOTT: Some members of one of the regular bands were in the habit of tiptoeing down at night to get milk to drink from the vending machine despite the place being alarmed directly to the fire brigade in Inverness. There was a lot going on behind the scenes that few knew about. The windows above the stage were hidden from general view but were used to observe the crowd. That office was also where the door money was counted.

When the dances came out there was a period of mayhem, likened by some to the Wild West, when travellers found the correct bus from the fleet of free buses while new acquaintances cemented their budding relationships. At the end of the night one of the bouncers would walk up and down with a wide broom sweeping the floor as the crowd dispersed. But that wasn't necessarily the end of the evening – there would be people wandering around waiting for lifts, looking for buses that had gone and emerging from all sorts of dark corners. A small police presence herded stragglers away from the Square.

The Pavilion also kept hold of one of those archaic rules – theirs stated that all groups had to consist of at least four members. That was normally okay, but even though Cream and Jimi Hendrix hadn't exploded on the music scene, the concept of the 'power trio' was very much bubbling under. They were also either cheaper to book or the members earned more, so someone was winning either way. But that rule is why, when a trio called 123 played in the Strath, they were known as the Four Spots and their manager mimed along on stage.

The Pathfinders were being hailed as 'Scotland's most exciting' group, but I never saw anything as astonishing as 'Beatstalkermania'. One time they tried to play a free concert for their fans in Glasgow's George Square – 400 people were expected and over 6000 turned up. The band had to be hurled onto police horses and galloped into the City Chambers for their own safety, and they were on the front page of every newspaper the next morning.

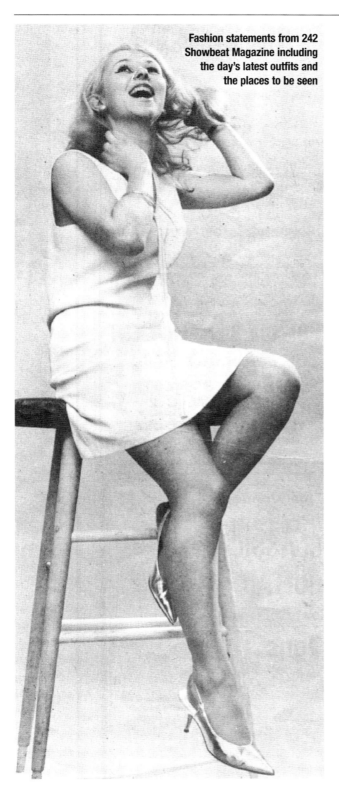

Fashion statements from 242 Showbeat Magazine including the day's latest outfits and the places to be seen

The Bo Weavles were witnesses to Beatstalkermania when we saw a hall full of screaming girls going mad ... to cardboard cut-outs of the band, who were in London at the time recording a record.

ALAN MAIR: The Beatstalkers had gone pro and we were doing very well. We'd bought a Z Cars car, the Zephyr 4. I used to never understand why people were staring at me – but I was seventeen, looked twelve, and I'm driving this really flashy car! We could go into McCormack's Music to buy expensive gear in cash, and we'd take even more cash in so we could wave it about and show off.

There were girls sleeping outside all our flats. I remember crawling across the floor from the bedroom to the kitchen, so they wouldn't see me through the front door window, just so I could have an hour to myself before the doorbell started ringing. One night there were 25 girls in the close. When you were with your wife or whatever it was hard going, because you never got a moment to yourself – but when you were with the band it was wonderful. The great thing is, it saw us through those problematic puberty years, when you don't know what to do with yourself.

We were so big in Scotland that we did a gig without even being there! They made cardboard cutouts of us, and put them on the revolving stage at the Dennistoun Palais, and the idea was Davie would phone the fans when the stage turned round. It's not like they didn't know they were going to see cardboard cutouts! It was billed as 'Not the Beatstalkers'. When Davie phoned it was put through the tannoy. Some of the girls who were there told me they'd been screaming at the cutouts, then when Davie's voice came over people started screaming louder, fainting and stuff like that!

Very little was famous in the Dennistoun Palais except the Calton Tongs. They infested it – there were hundreds of them and they dominated it from the 60s to its death. It wasn't terribly violent because one gang dominated. You'd get the odd fight if someone came in and didn't know them, but you didn't get many gang fights, certainly not that I heard of. But the Duke Street Palace was huge, incredibly popular and not as violent as the Barrowlands.

But that night was crazy, in a very good way – the Bo Weavles played, the stage rotated to reveal the cut-outs and the crowd went wild. Gordon Knowles, the manager, appealed for order: 'Calm down, we're waiting for the phone call!' The phone rang: 'Hello, it's Davie here!' And the crowd went wild. That's what people had paid to see. It went on for half an hour and everyone went home happy.

EDDIE JOHNSTON: The Hi Fi Combo had a really good fan base, like a family. I remember being quite blasé about signing autographs for the girls, but I imagine this was a result of my tender age. The manager always insisted it was part of being a pop star, although I never ever felt like anything other than a musician in a very good band. The fans would also turn up at the music shops and bars we frequented, as if by accident, and their lives seemed to revolve around the Hi Fi Combo.

We'd often pass many of the girls hitching to our gig, and give them a toot. If they were really lucky, we'd jam as many as possible into the back of the van beside the gear on the way home. We'd drop them off in Glasgow, at George Square, then head to a night club, usually the Picasso. Sometimes, the next day, without warning and usually at an unearthly hour, some of the girls would find their way to my parents' house. My father would shout, "Eddie, there are some wee lassies here from Glasgow – get out of bed!' I'd be obliged to sit up chatting to them before they'd go home. They'd done a round trip of sixty miles just for an hour's chat and a cup of tea.

The Bo Weavles enjoyed our own version of fan mania – including one memorable night in the Queen's Hall, Dunoon, which resulted in a near-death experience and a surprise bonus prize. We played there for Littlewood's Pools, and 300 women came to it. They all went wild, decided they wanted the band, and tried to attack the stage. The hallkeeper had to turn the fire hose on them. That same night we noticed there was a very high-quality velvet curtain there, and we decided to take it for cleaning after the water damage from the hose. When we'd cleaned it, I don't think they wanted it back. Certainly no one contacted us and asked for their curtain back. So that's how the Bo Weavles wound up with matching velvet suits.

The only other thing Dunoon had was a little club on the pier, which was run by Brian Wilson, who became an MP. He'd started out as entertainment convener at Glasgow University where he learned communism – and this communist hardliner wouldn't pay me more than £25 for a band ...

The arrival of pirate radio in Scotland was incredibly useful to the new music scene. Before Radio Scotland started broadcasting from the Comet, a lightship anchored in international waters, the only pop music you could hear on the radio in Scotland was half an hour a week on the BBC, or Radio Luxembourg at night, which only played 30-second clips of records. Some people were fortunate enough to be able to hear the US Army's AFN service, but that only made them more aware of how poor Scotland's domestic offering was.

Radio Scotland changed all that. Not only was there a full-time pop station, the government couldn't control it as long as it was broadcasting offshore. So it was dangerous as well as exciting. Before long, a lot of the DJs were household names – especially Stuart Henry, because he suffered chronic seasickness and had to stay on dry land. Instead, he made a lot of personal appearances around the country to promote Radio Scotland, and fronted a lot of their popular Clan Balls, which were always great fun.

DOUG CARMICHAEL: The Comet in the summer was a brilliant experience – although on the first couple of days I had to be relieved in the studio because of seasickness ... It did take time to get used to the motion of a ship anchored three miles off the coast. But the craic on board was great.

On Sunday afternoons we'd all lie nearly naked on the deck and fishing boats would come out with tourists and fans who wanted to see the ship. They always brought us presents – for instance, if someone mentioned on air that we liked chocolate cake, that's what they'd bring us!

JOHN KERR: I also remember many pop stars coming out to visit when they were playing Scotland – Cat Stevens and Gene Pitney were regulars. Once I got fairly excited about an upcoming visit from an Australian star, Normie Rowe. I'd compered a lot of his shows so I'd been bragging to all the DJs about this tall, good-looking guy – I knew what a star he was, especially with the girls. He's still very popular today. Normie arrived out on the Comet's tender on a pretty rough sea day, stepped on board and promptly threw up on the deck. So much for the macho star I'd been portraying ...

DOUG CARMICHAEL: Radio Scotland had a huge, loyal, following. The Clan Balls, especially at the Locarno in Glasgow, were hugely supported – especially when the Troggs starred, when there were people jumping onstage cuddling DJs, groups and everyone else. The kids wanted anything that was Radio Scotland – you had to make sure your trousers had a belt!

I managed Stuart Henry, who was always likened to a Scottish Jimmy Savile and he was amazingly popular with all age groups. I lived in the flat below his, and fans always seemed to find out his address, and they'd camp outside till he made an appearance.

SANDRA COLL: To my shame I was one of the many girls who used to wait outside Stuart Henry's flat in the hope he'd come by and I could meet him. Sure enough, one night he turned up and I handed him a piece of paper for an autograph. While I stood there, to my embarrassment I passed wind really quite loudly. I must have been nervous! Stuart burst out laughing and said, 'Hey, did you just fart?' I told him it was my shoes had just squeaked and he looked horrified and said sorry for being so rude to me. That was close!

Not only was Radio Scotland making a noise on air – the station was also publishing a monthly magazine, *242 Showbeat*, which was another very useful outlet for the new groups on the scene. The country was very well-served – there was also *Transplant Magazine*, *Moody* and the *Lennoxbank News* which became *Beat News*, so it was quite easy to get the word out.

GORDON HUNTER: We fixed the *Lennoxbank News* top-ten chart once ... There was a band called the Trackers which was made up of apprentices from

Radio Scotland's Stuart Henry and Cathy Spence interview Adam Faith for the station

Rolls-Royce in Hillington. You had to write in to vote for your band so loads of us from Rolls-Royce wrote in for the Trackers – and they got to number one.

ARTHUR SCOTT: By the mid 60s the Strath had caught up with other venues in the north and featured some well-known names such as the Merseybeats, Kenny Ball and his Jazzmen and Brian Poole and the Tremeloes. But the best period of all, in my opinion, came in 1967.

The bill featured Freddie and the Dreamers, Stuart Henry, Millie, the Poets, the Rockin' Berries, Whistlin' Jack Smith, the Nashville Teens and the Fortunes. These were all artistes who had appeared on TV and radio. The Fortunes in particular were absolutely fantastic and their standout number in the act was 'I Was Made to Love Her', a cover of a recent hit by Stevie Wonder.

The end of 1967 saw the beginning of the residency of the Sterling Showband. They were to remain for about 18 months during which time they built up a loyal fan base. Everyone looked forward to their version of 'Please Stay' by the Crying Shames, since it provided you with at least one chance of actually getting your arms round someone.

Irish showbands were something of a phenomenon at the time. Some of us believed in putting on a real show but a lot of acts weren't doing that. So when you added a little of the Irish charm to a band who were paying attention to what they did on stage while they played, you had a recipe for some very happy dancers. The Strathpeffer Pavilion's Irish outfit, the Sterling Showband, changed their name to the Galaxy Showband towards the end of their tenure there. Sadly a road accident was to make an impression on that dance hall for the second time.

TOM POYNTON: With a few showbands behind me at 23 years of age I was fortunate enough to be offered the job of lead singer with the Galaxy Showband from Lurgan.

I landed at Inverness airport a week after the rest of the band had headed over for the residency in Scotland, and I was picked up by the sax player and lead gutarist, and taken to the Strath.

My first impressions of the building were of its size and remoteness. The ballroom itself was spacious, the stage was a good size and the lighting and acoustics were very good. There was even a separate little bar in the hall which was used nightly by the locals and ourselves.

I was shown up to a room at the very top of the Strath and told: 'This is your room'. It was clean but sparse – a single bed, a wardrobe and a chest of drawers with a couple of pictures on the wall.

Readers' Top Ten groups.

1. BEATSTALKERS
2. GAYLORDS
3. POETS
4. BO-WEAVLES
5. PATHFINDERS
6. STUDIO SIX
7. HIPPLE PEOPLE
8. MERIDIANS
9. SOL BYRON and the SENATE
10. SABRES

Compiled by the readers of MOODY.

But when I lay down for the night I got a feeling of a presence in the room. I couldn't sleep – then after a few hours of tossing and turning I saw a strange dark outline of a figure cross the room. I saw it twice again that night, and needless to say I was frightened ...

At breakfast the next morning the cook asked me if I had slept okay. Not wanting to be taken for a wimp I said I had. She said, 'Did ye no' see the ghost? That top room's haunted!'

Straight after breakfast another lad and I went up and packed my gear. I got a bed in another room with three of the rest of the band and I never went up there again.

After playing to packed houses at the Strath and making friends with a few of the locals I was sad when I left, but I was looking forward to seeing my family back in Belfast for Christmas.

Our coach overturned in a blizzard just south of Inverness – the coach and our gear were completely wrecked, but thankfully everyone escaped serious injury. But it was the end of the Galaxy – we disbanded when we got back to Ireland and I haven't seen any of the band or been back to the Strath since. I'd love to go back. You never know ...

Nobody told us it was haunted when we stayed there. But we got done by the police on the way home – we were in a Ford Zephyr owned by a guy called Davey Crockett, but the tyres weren't legal. So we were checked over by the police and I was asked: 'Whose car is this?' And I told him: 'Davey Crockett's.' The policeman took an attitude right away: 'Oh aye, smart bastard, are ye?' Fortunately there was a letter in the car addressed to Davey. He had to believe me then, although he wasn't happy about it.

MARTIN GRIFFITHS: The System's big chance came when we managed to get a gig at the Flamingo Ballroom, Paisley Road, backing the famous Pathfinders.

They were magnificent. I remember waiting outside after one of their gigs at Clarkston Hall. There was a bunch of girls hanging around their van, and just before they set off there came a voice from inside: 'If ye fuck ye can jump in!' And to my innocent amazement most of the girls did! Jump in, I mean ...

We even hired a bus to take the fans from our school to support us. The ballroom was huge, with an enormous flamingo strung from the ceiling. Even the smell of the room was electifying – that strong smell of excitement was everywhere. We used the Pathfinders' equipment and it was the first time I'd sung through a decent mike.

The Pathfinders were magnificent and we saw and heard how a professional band worked. They played soul standards their way and Clewsy was the perfect frontman – he was way ahead of his time. Offstage he was a very quiet man, but once up and running he became a big brash personality, oozing with confidence.

To us they were just the epitome of what a group should be. The manager of the ballroom told us to give up – but I'm glad I didn't.

Keeping it lively: Radio Scotland's magazine was an important part of the nation's scene for two short years, promoting stars of the circuit alongside its own Clan Balls like the one in Dundee below

RADIO SCOTLAND'S SHOWBEAT MONTHLY

YAK
MOONIES
ALP

EXCLUSIVE!

242 MEETS BATMAN

ALEX HARVEY EXPOSES SHOWBIZ SHARKS

A MERRY CHRISTMAS FROM RADIO SCOTLAND

242 SHOWBEAT MONTHLY

CHEVLONS — STUDIO SIX — CHRIS McCLURE

242 SHOWBEAT
RADIO SCOTLAND'S MONTHLY

1/-

Vol. 1   No. 7   OCTOBER, 1966

STOICS EXTRA

MAC THE KNIFE

STAR PIX

BO-WEAVLES — THREE'S A CROWD
ZOOT MONEY — CATHY SPENCE PICTURE
SPECIAL — LONDON STYLE LATEST

BEATSTALKRAZY!

Police lose caps —and control—as fans go berserk

BY
CORINNE
CLARK

POP blew up yesterday. Like B-A-N-G! An explosion of teenage hysteria that rocked Glasgow's Kinning Park.

★

At the centre of the blast was the city's own pop group The Beatstalkers.

Scores of police lost their caps and all control of the hundreds of frenzied girls who went berserk and Beatstalkrazy.

★

There to open a mods and rockers shop in Lambhill Street, the group had to fight through 300 girl fans before singer Davie Lennon of Priesthill collapsed on the shop

Fan goes...out

floor — and had to receive treatment later at the Southern General Hospital.

Eddie McCullough (21), who owns the shop suffered a badly cut wrist as he tried to keep the fans from stampeding.

Later he looked amazed at the deep cut and said: "I don't know how I came by it.

As the group toured the shop, excited teenage girls banged with

their fists against the windows and several burst through the police barriers.

One dark - haired, head - scarved girl enthusiastically kissed each of the group in

turn. A blonde, who had been carried half-conscious into the shop after collapsing in the crowd recovered sufficiently to shake hands reverently with each of her idols.

The Beatstalkers accepted the stramash nonchalantly.

"A great 'reception," commented 16-year-old Allan Mair, as he loosened his tie preparatory to battling his way back to the car again.

★

● The Beatstalkers did a hectic hour-long session at the Dennistoun Palais last night . . . minus lead singer Davie Lennon, who collapsed earlier when the group visited Kinning Park.

Said manager Joe Gaffney: "Davie was badly shaken up by the incident today and along with that is suffering from flu. He felt he could not

Sgt. goe

Beatstalker goes...over

Anything goes...in grip of fan hysteria

Pictures by James

The Beatstalkers' fan hysteria challenged Beatlemania of two years earlier

They're really a riot

9 He started tooting the horn – they'd got their dental braces tangled

IT'S DIFFICULT to believe now, but until the mid-60s the charts were counted by sales of sheet music rather than records. That wasn't the only massive change in the big wide world, of course. The Rolling Stones took over from the Beatles as the 'worst' influence on teenagers. The goverment introduced legislation which closed down the short-lived and very successful pirate radio phenomenon, launching BBC Radio One in its place. The beat bands dominated the scene in Scotland, with the Forth Road Bridge and other improvements in infrastructure making travel a little easier. So everybody went further afield.

CATH McDONALD: The Picasso Club in Glasgow was a tiny place, but all the bands would gather there after they'd played wherever they'd been playing. There was a lull after the first band and the main band because we could never find the DJs, Tom Ferrie or Alex Robertson – because the two of them were drunk somewhere. The DJ box was up a set of ladders – not steps, ladders – so you had to push the guys up to get them into the box. (Later on you'd just let them fall down the ladders.)

So in that lull, if the Dream Police were playing they'd do something funny. They came in with a pantomime horse once – two in the costume, one sitting on it, one leading it, and they went out of the club, stopped a bus and got on it, all in the horse outfit. They only paid two tickets and the guy shouted, 'What about they two?' and the band said, 'I don't know – what do you charge for horses?'

One night I came in and I thought the Pathfinders were playing until I saw the singer, Ian Clews, coming up the stairs. He said, 'Who's that playing?' I said, 'I thought it was you!' – so we took a look and it was the Dream Police imitating the Pathfinders, doing all their songs and making a fool of them. There was a rivalry, but it was fun and it never got out of hand ...

Sometimes the Picasso went on till 6 but usually stopped at 3, then we went on to the Ram Jam Club which was open till 6 or 7 every morning.

The last two years of the 1960s were marked by the first real terror story in the history of the dancin' – Bible John. Very little was known about the reality behind the scaremongering. What is known is that three girls were found murdered after nights out in Glasgow, and the one name in common was a person called John who quoted the Bible and said he didn't drink at Hogmanay, but instead he said prayers. The police were desperate to track him down but after months of manhunting nothing was ever discovered.

ALEX LINDSAY: During Bible John's reign of terror almost every 20th couple dancing in the Barrowlands were plain-clothes police. You could spot them by their size 12 shoes.

The truth is a lot of the scaremongering was all made up. Three murders is a sobering thought – but that's not what was on people's minds. The Barrowland, the Plaza and the Majestic were getting all the publicity. When the papers said: 'Police spoke to 1000 people at the Plaza' you thought: 'That place sounds busy – I'd better go for a dance there.' You'd think there was nowhere else to dance.

We were running Bible John lookalike nights, and Be Bible John For A Night contests. At no time did it affect any crowd anywhere. It's not as if everyone expected to be murdered – that didn't occur to people. It was treated very lightly and in some of the trendy city clubs it was just a joke.

I think, as an operator, how you read the papers is different from how you hope the punters are going to read it. It was good news for the premises. If they say, someone's going to die this Friday, then it'll be quiet. But if they say someone's about called Bible John, 'Aye that'll be right,' and everyone's joking about it.

I think the papers didn't know how to make it really sensational. There was someone who murdered people on the A1 – the A1 could have been on Mars for people in Scotland. So they tried to make their Bible John coverage sound like the A1 murderer, except it was happening on your doorstep. We couldn't have cared less. Bible John – what a great name! He could have been a disc jockey ...

ARCHIE YOUNG: There was no proper training or licence to operate as a doorman in those days. I trained with an amateur football team to stay fit and fast-moving. An old chap gave me great advice – he told me to watch the eyes because that always gave people away and you'd know what they were about to do. He also told me to stand sideways to make me harder to hit, and he was right enough.

Sometimes your job was just to help people. One night a patron had trouble starting his Hillman Imp outside the Cavendish, so I went to help him use the starting-handle. The Imp's engine was at the back, which was unusual, so of course the hole for the starting-handle was there too. I was turning the handle like God knows what when a policeman appeared and asked if I was drinking –

he got another officer over and they were going to do me with drunk driving until I explained the engine was at the back and it wasn't my car anyway. His face went red and his pal was laughing his head off. It always pays to check the facts!

Another time a couple had stopped their car opposite the dance hall. They were kissing like mad in the front and we were keeping half an eye on them when the guy started tooting the horn like crazy. I went over to see what was wrong. It turned out they both had dental braces and they'd got tangled! We had to get the police who somehow managed to get them free.

ALEX LINDSAY: I was also a bouncer in the Plaza, where one night there was a bang and a cloud of dust. A figure came flying down from above and landed on the dance floor. It was a young man who'd been stripping the lead from the roof.

CAMERON DRUMMOND: I heard they asked him where he came from – and he replied: 'Up there ...'

Back in the land of music, the Beatles had changed everything again with *Sgt Pepper's Lonely Hearts Club Band*. Added together with Cream and Jimi Hendrix, there was a whole new texture developing, and it spoke to a lot of people in Scotland. There was the Summer of Love and Woodstock – and of course, drugs were beginning to make an appearance.

PETE AGNEW: Manny Charlton played with the Red Hawks, then they went modern and changed their name to the Marshmallow 400 – a great move, oh my God! We were playing across at the Bellville Hotel because we'd fallen out with the Kinema at the time. He used to finish a little bit later than us so we'd usually go and get him and we'd all go for a fish supper. But that night he arrived at our gig before we finished. He said: 'We got fired!'

There'd been a bus in from Glasgow and the keyboard player had started playing a song. Manny had no idea what it was, so he just joined in playing the chords. Manny said: 'I'm just banging away and next thing you know it was complete mayhem. So they sacked us for playing this song. What's "The Sash"?' So the Marshmallow 400 broke up and Manny ended up playing with the Tommy Samson Orchestra at the Raith Ballroom for six months before joining us.

The pop bands, the Tremeloes or whatever, would play about half an hour but bands like the Who, which was called underground in those days, they'd do an hour or more, which of course we liked.

Chicken Shack had just released 'Maudie', which was a good wee song. We'd been playing it for weeks so we thought we'd do it as a wee tribute to them, but Stan Webb went mental because Chicken Shack didn't do it! The crowd are shouting for it and he went: 'Well you can hear from they bastards when they come back on!' (You used to have to play before and after.)

The new heavy rock movement appealed to the band that had been the Bo Weavles. We were quite soft and it was perceived to be out of date. We'd recorded one song, Summer Sands, but drugs weren't involved in its creation and that showed – it was so bad.

> **DAVE BATCHELOR:** 'Summer sands beneath my feet, footsteps all around' ... etcetera, etcetera. The big mistake came when bands started writing their own material. Because for most of them that's what it was: a mistake!

The bands killed the scene for themselves. They got too clever – they got too musical, forgot about dressing up, putting a show on and playing music you could dance to. They'd all learned from the Isley Brothers, the Four Tops and acts like that – immaculate presentation, but bands here decided to go grungy. That satisfied an element of the audience but it didn't satisfy people who wanted to dance and maybe get a lumber. What they were doing was great if you really wanted to be a musician, but most of them really just wanted to have fun and meet girls.

Of course, it worked out well for some of us. We became Tear Gas, often known as 'Fear Gas', because of our volume. And we were very loud – especially by the time we'd wound up with the big lineup: Dave Batchelor on vocals, Zal Cleminson on guitar, Hugh McKenna on keys, Chris Glen on bass and Ted McKenna on drums.

A few years later this would be the sensational band that backed Alex Harvey, with Dave staying on in a production role. Meanwhile, the Shadettes were soon to become Nazareth and head down the 'head music' road as well.

> **PETE AGNEW:** We played in the Royal Hotel, Fraserburgh, just at the time of 'Whole Lotta Love'. Everyone was starting to bang their guitars off mic stands and that was supposed to be cool. But it was still supposed to be the dancin' ... So we're up, banging away, and the punters were all standing watching because you can't dance to 'Whole Lotta Love'. So we went to get paid – forty quid, which was good money – and Jimmy Ritchie comes over, gives me the money and says: 'Well son, I'm gonna tell ye, you're the worst band I've ever seen in my life. Would you like some tea and sandwiches?'
>
> About six weeks later we were up doing the Aberdeenshire weekend – Aberdeen, Aviemore and Fraserburgh – so we're back in Fraserburgh and the place was mobbed. So I said to Jimmy: 'I thought we were the worst band you'd ever seen in your life?' He said: 'Aye, but they couldn't believe it the first time ...'

A lot of big acts were warming to the idea that you could test your tour out on the Scottish audiences before taking it to places they felt were more important, like London or the USA. Albert Bonici had made good money out of the London belief that Scotland was a village, which had got him that exclusive Beatles deal. Now the crowds up north were being treated to longer shows with more experimental songs and performances, as the bands refined what they did before presenting it round the world. And no one was complaining because it meant in Scotland you got more for your ticket price.

Although Roger Waters did complain about the size of some stages during Pink Floyd's 1969 tour of Scotland, which meant they were unable to put on their full lighting display at places like the Two Red Shoes. He said one day the band would travel round with their own circus tent in the future. In a way, they did.

BRIAN NOBILE: David Bowie played the Kinema Ballroom's Folk Club the night after he did his proper gig there on a Sunday night. He'd been meant to be playing in Stirling but it was cancelled, so he made a guest appearance at the Folk Club on the Tuesday instead. John Watt, of Kelty Clippie fame, booked all the acts and he thought Bowie was a better folk singer than he was a pop singer.

Kinema Ballroom

TONIGHT (FRIDAY):
THE CHANGE
plus THE SHADETTES
8 pm to 1 am.   Admission 5/-, after 9 pm 7/-.   Late Transport.

SATURDAY
THE CHANGE
THE PHOENIX
THE SHADETTES
Admission 5/-, after 9 pm 7/-.   Late Transport.
Every Saturday Afternoon Dancing for the Young
with
THE PHOENIX
1 to 3 pm.   Admission 2/-.

SUNDAY:
DAVID BOWIE and JUNIOR'S EYES
plus
THE SHADETTES
8 pm to 11 pm.   Admission 7/-.

KB FOLK CLUB: TUESDAY, 11th November:
ARCHIE FISHER

PETE AGNEW: Cecil Hunter at the Kinema had no idea what bands to book so he'd always take the ones who were in the top ten or top twenty, and he wasn't getting great crowds. So we told him, get Spooky Tooth, get Deep Purple – but he hadn't heard of them. So he got Deep Purple and sold the place out, about 900 people, and he couldn't believe it.

The Who came up and did *Tommy*, which no one had heard at this point. But Cecil was a right wee dictator – the Who were on stage playing and he sent one of the bouncers down to tell them to turn it down because he couldn't hear Scotsport!

BRIAN NOBILE: Everybody that night was thrilled by what they were hearing and the band was really cooking. But downstairs Cecil was pulling his hair out trying to get a picture on his black and white TV. Scotsport was coming on with highlights of the Pars game but because of the Who's electrical interference and sound levels he couldn't get a picture, and couldn't hear anything if he did. So he had to make a decision – and he later told me it had been an easy one to make. He sent one of his staff up to say if the Who didn't turn it down he'd pull the plug on the band and put the Shadettes back on.

PETE AGNEW: When they finished it was ten to eleven, and the place shut at eleven so we thought: 'Ach, we'll no' bother ... Pete Townshend has just smashed two guitars and the place has gone mental – we'll leave it.' But Cecil was like: 'Get up there, you've got ten minutes to play.'

Scene to be seen in: the Picasso Club in Glasgow, where bands would gather after their shows

So we were up playing and all our pals are walking out the exits on either side of the stage going: 'Who do you think you are, the Who?' We didn't want to be doing it – we were told to do it. So we played before the Who and after them, before Spooky Tooth and after them, before Deep Purple and after them ... It was kind of embarrassing actually, but it was good to see the bands.

Men like Cecil Hunter, with many years' experience of ballrooms but no great understanding of the new era, were, sadly, drifting into history – taking some wonderful characters with them. If I, and people like me, represented the new era of management, and if Ronnie Simpson represented the next generation of agents, Sandy McBaine was one man who exemplified the kind of person who'd keep a ballroom alive.

The Olympia in East Kilbride had only opened in 1960, but almost the moment the Beatles exploded it began suffering from a failure to embrace the changes which had taken place around it. Sandy became its manager at 22 years of age in the middle of the decade and set about turning it round.

He was featured in *Moody* magazine, the publication 'for Scotland's with-it set' as a go-getter who frequently worked until 4am. An article explained: *The day of the dinner jacket was over; what was needed was someone who thought as the young and who was as "with-it" as the "with-it" set. Sandy, full of bounce and effervescence, has set out to make the Olympia the centre of beat, and he looks as if he has every likelihood of succeeding.*

'He must be one of the few ballroom managers in Britain known personally by almost all of his customers. He thinks nothing of people coming up and saying to him, "Here, Sandy, how about getting the Walker Brothers up for us?"

'He has made it clear he is interested in THEM and their likes. If they want the Walker Brothers then by golly he will get them – or do his hardest anyway. He is not afraid to spend money as long as he gets what he wants, or rather what you want.'

Thinking like that is what it took for ballrooms to survive – they had, and to this day still have, to provide what people want rather than insisting they already know. Anyone who didn't make the grade saw their grand old hall close down – and sadly many people saw exactly that. But as Ronnie Simpson says: 'Guys, we're sorry. It wasn't us. It was just the way it had to be.'

DAVE VALENTINE: The Hipple People were excited about supporting the Who in Magoo's. But after we'd played two hours and they still hadn't appeared, someone said we'd better give the crowd at least a taste of them, so we launched into a version of 'Can't Explain', then left the stage – only to come face-to-face with the real thing, who'd been watching us from the wings. Oops! They did a great show and it's good to have seen them starting to fly onto greater things, although Pete Townshend couldn't manage to break his guitar at the end and he was furious!

In those days all the name acts were well-received. Even Chris Farlowe was

OLYMPIA BALLROOM
EAST KILBRIDE
Scotland's Big Beat Ballroom
TOP STARS SWINGING YOUR WAY AT OLYMPIA SOON

| THE HOLLIES | LULU | THE ANIMALS |
| THE WALKER BROS. | THE ROCKIN' BERRIES | THE YARDBIRDS |

Friday, 8 p.m. till 1 a.m.
THE LATE NITE
Music to suit all age groups by the fabulous KIMBOS SHOWBAND and TARDY HOST BEAT GROUP
ADMISSION — 6/0d.
Late Transport to Glasgow and Hamilton

Sat., 7.30 till 11.30 p.m.
THE BIG STAR NITE
Dance and listen to the above star names plus the fabulous KIMBOS SHOWBAND
ADMISSION — 8/6d.
Late transport to Glasgow and Hamilton

Sun., 7.30 till 10.30 p.m.
THE TEEN NITE
SPIRITS, TARDY HOST and other fab groups
ADMISSION — 3/0d.

Mon., 7.30 till 10.30 p.m.
THE TEEN BEAT NITE
Featuring the TARDY HOST and THE SPIRITS
ADMISSION — 3/0d.

Tuesday, open 7 p.m. eyes down 8 p.m.
BINGO AND SOCIAL CLUB
Snowball £100 up — Jackpot £40 up
FREE MEMBERSHIP.
ADMISSION — 2/6d.

Wednesday & Thursday
PRIVATE FUNCTIONS
Staff Dances, etc.
Apply Manager — E.K. 22286

Saturday, 2 till 4.30 p.m.
Afternoon RECORD ROUNDUP
Featuring East Kilbride's own JIMMY ("KENNY") SAVILLE
ADMISSION — 2/0d.

FOR FURTHER DETAILS PHONE SANDY McBAINE, MANAGER, EAST KILBRIDE 22286

Sandy McBaine worked hard to put the Olympia on the map

hauled off the stage by screaming girls – and he was no oil painting. All the top Glasgow bands came through as well: the Pathfinders, the Poets, Studio Six, House of Lords and the regular Jimmy James and the Vagabonds.

DEN BAIRD: My pal Jocky refused to come and see the Who because he didn't think there'd be much talent at the show. That was when I realised some people were into the music and some people couldn't care less!

DAVE VALENTINE: The Hipple People had a near-residency at the International in Edinburgh, which was run by Dave Roccio. He was constantly getting complaints about the noise from the venue so he installed a noise limiter, which would cut off the power if the volume reached a certain level. The problem was he pretended it wasn't there, and that caused a bit of a running battle because limiters were capable of knackering your amps.

One night one of our amps went live. I turned to see our guitarist Jim was screaming in pain – he'd been thrown in the air but he couldn't release his grip on his guitar. I managed to jump over the piano and yank the plugs out of the wall. Fortunately he wasn't seriously burned and I think we were even able to continue the show. A narrow escape indeed.

Jimmy Bain, the bassist with Three's A Crowd, had a party-piece where he'd rush to one side of the stage, drop his drawers and light his farts. He seemed

to enjoy people watching as the large flame issued from his bum. Strange
boy – but he went on to play in Ritchie Blackmore's Rainbow.

The International became a gay disco called Fire Island, then it burned down,
so it was well-named ...

The International was a scary place to play. It was owned by a gangster, and if someone said that in those days you actually believed it was Al Capone. I have no idea what the owner looked like, but the stories were scary. You played it and got out as fast as you could, but it was a busy club.

LENNY TOSHACK: Other decent clubs in Edinburgh included the Gonk, the International or Nash and the Green Light at Morningside. Probably the best club at the end of the golden era was Romanos at the west end of Princes Street. That's where I first cut my teeth as a DJ. It was a superb club that had a bar for the first time.

Mecca, who owned a lot of dance halls all over Britain, decided to create a brand of hall known as Tiffany's. A lot of places took that name and were designed to a similar format, with palm trees in the foyer. That's what happened to the Locarno in Glasgow – I saw it at the tail-end of its best years, then it degenerated into the most violent place in the city when it became Tiffany's.

It had been famous for its bands – Maggie Bell and Lulu sang there, and other great singers and great bands. It had opened in 1936 and had the first revolving stage in Scotland. It made its name during the war when the Americans and Canadians attended the Locarno, and the Shore Patrol used to go in and they were very violent. It's probably fair to say it was more notorious than loved.

But Cream played there, and there was a Staxx show – Otis Redding, Sam and Dave, Eddie Floyd, Booker T and the MGs all played to an alleged 5000-strong crowd. And I had Deep Purple in there, the night they closed Sauchiehall Street.

Derek Nicol had booked them for £500 and they went to the top of the charts with 'Black Night'. We hadn't put the tickets on sale for the Electric Garden, capacity 1200. So we quickly booked the Locarno and said, we don't have time to do any more tickets so we'll sell the 1200 then we'll take the walk-up. (Glasgow has always been known on the touring circuit as a city with a good walk-up – people prefer to buy on the door on the night rather than in advance.)

On the night of the gig a queue built that was so big it closed the street. The police turned up on horses and announced: 'Anyone without a ticket leave the street.' My walk-up! My money! I was chasing a policeman on a horse shouting, 'No! No!' But he said: 'You're not closing a street in my city.'

We'd built a special stage for Deep Purple – they'd turned up and told us the stage was too long and too low. We got a specification and promised to build it by five o'clock. They said: 'Do it or we're not going on.' There was a big not-going-on thing – they were at the top of the charts and didn't want to play for just £500. They didn't want to be here when America was screaming for them.

Tear Gas went on before them and did a great set. Wonderful – I loved it. And then Deep Purple just blew us away. I still can't believe it. The volume, clarity, the ability – it all left me speechless.

PETE AGNEW: You had to remember you were still playing in a dance hall – you had to play things people could still dance to. It wasn't until we went through to the Electric Garden that you started noticing punters who were just standing watching the bands instead of doing anything else. Most were still dancing – you'd still hear someone shouting, 'Hey pal, a slow one!' Okay, someone's trying to get a lumber here, so we'll do 'Please Stay'. You'd try to do four jumpy-about songs then do a slow one so people could get a cuddle.

1970s

As live acts explored music you couldn't dance to, the DJ's record decks became the main source of moving sounds – with help from better speaker systems

BEAT ROOM TO BOOTH BOOM

10 This is a farce – pick one girl or two and get rid of the rest

THE MUSIC of Freda Payne, I'd say – Band of Gold and all that – was tested on someone with a wooden leg. They'd play him the record and say, 'Can you dance to that?' and if he hobbled about quite happily they'd know it would be a hit.

But the rock movement started happening in a big way – Black Sabbath, Deep Purple, Led Zeppelin, with Zeppelin leading the charge. In Scotland Mustard had become Tear Gas, the Shadettes became Nazareth and all the bands went heavy rock. The beginning of the 1970s was important to rock music.

> **COLIN ROBERTSON:** But the punter didn't want to dance to it. The two things a punter hated most was a drum solo or a guitar solo. But in the Electric Garden we still knew how to keep the audience entertained. Ronnie Simpson was good at predicting which singles would do well. He could say, 'That song will go to number one in six weeks' and we'd book the band for that week. He was right a lot of the time. We had Thunderclap Newman playing for £50 when they were at number one with 'Something in the Air'.

There was also Joanna's in Glasgow, one of the best early discos and very difficult to get into because of the demand, unless you were among the favoured few. It was a fabulous club, run by Max Langon below the Albert Hall. It was the first one to be licenced, but to drink you had to eat, so you were given spam and chips, and it was compulsory to consume at least one chip. If someone came in and caught you without your spam and chips we were all in trouble. That was the law. A quarter tonne of chips, half a tonne of spam, and splat onto paper plates.

The White Elephant was another success story and another spam-and-chips place. When it opened the owner of Unicorn Leisure, Frank Lynch, posed with an elephant and the papers ran the headline 'Elephant Man' – how creative is that! It was popular with a slightly older crowd. Footballers went there. Jimmy Johnstone, Dixie Deans and many others were barred for drinking and causing trouble. It was based on illegal functions, feeding people spam and chips to serve drink. The functions were all made up – if you had a man who said he worked at Rolls-Royce, it was a Rolls-Royce workers function that night!

As Aberdeen commentator Peter Innes once observed, the drinking ritual in places which were licensed early was a familiar one: *'Six-deep, trying anything to attract the attention of uncaring, amateur and undermanned bar staff, in order to buy warm and overpriced alcohol in plastic glasses. Woe betide the fool who was careless enough to appear a wee bit boozy. The only female interested was likely to have a thirst like a warehouse full of blotting paper – and then enter the dreaded bouncers ...'*

But places like Joanna's and the White Elephant worked on that and improved the service. It had the first-ever female DJ in Britain — Julie, Max Langdon's girlfriend, and there had never been one before. She was a fabulous DJ and it really helped create an atmosphere, because when people came in to see the first woman DJ she really played on it.

ANNE MORGAN: We could never get into Joanna's, no matter how hard we tried. Then one night I overheard a couple of other girls telling the bouncer they were friends of the DJ. The bouncer went to get the DJ and I realised the girls didn't know if it was going to work, because they didn't really know him! Sure enough, this blonde good-looking guy came out, looked them up and down, winked and and said, 'Yeah, they're with me.' I shouted: 'Us too – you remember me, don't you?' and he laughed and let us in. I wonder how many other people he let in whenever he felt like it ...

ROSE MASTERTON: For an example of simpler times, this always makes me laugh – a couple of girls I knew managed to get into the Kinema to interview Elton John by pretending they were journalists with the *Dunfermline Press* ... They didn't even have notebooks or a camera, but the bouncers let them in and took them to Elton's dressing room, where he was very nice to them and gave them a cup of tea before sending them on their way!

TOMMY PATERSON: If you think those 1970s sitcoms were far-fetched you should have seen the trouble my pal Gordy used to get himself into. He was a tall, good-looking feller and he earned a few quid so he could give a girl a good night at the dancin'. Trouble was, he couldn't go into the Olympia in East Kilbride without trying to give more than one girl a good night. One night I was trying to keep five different lassies from realising he was going with them all, in the same room at the one time. I told him, 'Gordy, you need to sort this farce out. Pick one, or two of them if you need to, and get rid of the rest,' He gave this wee lost boy look and said: 'I can't do that, Tommy – I love them all!' He never did settle down ...

LAURA CAMPBELL: We had a Canadian exchange student staying with us, a

lovely girl called Nuala. She was a bit of a looker so I was a little bit apprehensive when I decided to take her to the dancin' in Stirling with me. Turns out I was right – not being from here, she stuck out like a sore thumb. The worst bit was she'd never had a drink before so after a few sips of cider before we went into the dance hall she was already in a bit of a state. Her glasses steamed up and she spent the night a complete mess – but even then a good Scots girl couldn't get any attention from the guys in the room, because Nuala was a novelty!

At the Electric Garden we at Unicorn were trying to build something special with an unforgettable atmosphere. One of the most important things which helped that happen came in the form of our DJ, Tim Stevens, who went on to become the legend that is Tiger Tim. He wasn't scared of anything and was a real personality, and that came to personify what the Electric Garden was. It's fair to say we championed the era of the personality club DJ, because the only other big names you had were radio jocks. It was a completely different job description but Tim fitted the bill perfectly.

TIGER TIM STEVENS: I was really excited because this was the big-time. I'd be on £3 a night, three nights a week, which is a bit more than I'd been making working full-time on the railways.

DJ Tony Meehan

I went along before my first night. I met the resident DJ, Tony Meehan. That was a thrill because he'd been on pirate Radio Scotland and played my first-ever request when I was younger. He invited me along to have a look before my first official night, and Edison Lighthouse were playing. Colin Robertson told me to introduce them but as I went on stage the female fans started screaming and grabbing onto my legs. I only made it to the safety of the DJ booth with the help of the bouncers but I thought, 'This is the life for me'.

MOIRA REDDIE: I met my husband at the Electric Garden. Not long after I'd started seeing him we were in the Gardens and he pointed at Tiger Tim and said, 'That's my cousin.' I didn't believe him but he said, 'No, really – his name's Jim McGrory.' I was well impressed – he knew a real-live celebrity! As it turns out they're third cousins and the families barely know each other, so I was never going to meet Tiger Tim through the man who became my husband.

But we loved the Gardens because you could listen and dance to live music like Tear Gas, the Dream Police, Slade and so on. The problem was we spent very little time there because, like many of my friends, I married at the very young age of 24. The habit of copying parents' traditions didn't change even though there was no war to encourage you to marry young! But we had to save up to buy a house because you couldn't get 100% mortgages, and courting outside the club scene was a lot cheaper, so that's what you did – you had to be selective as to what you attended.

CATH McDONALD: The first night I worked in the Electric Garden someone hit me from behind and knocked me out ... Eddie claims it was a standard trick to see if the staff were committed enough to keep coming back!

When Slade played we always had to come in at least an hour early. And the doors were closed by the time we should have been opening because you couldn't get any more people in.

At the end of the night we all wanted to go on somewhere else so we used to get some of the boys from Slade to help out in the ladies cloakroom. When word got round that Slade were there the girls all came to collect their coats and the hall emptied quicker.

COLIN ROBERTSON: There are people who still believe they saw Elvis Presley in the Electric Garden. Frank Lynch booked Raving Rupert, who's still going, and we put posters up saying 'Appearing at the Electric Garden' but didn't say who it was. So he came on in the Elvis gear – he's from Scunthorpe but he really did look and sound like Elvis. So when he said: 'Thank you very much, it's great to be here in Glas-*gow*,' people really thought it was Elvis. They went home saying, 'I never thought I'd see Elvis in Glasgow.' We never told them otherwise.

On the other hand, if a band were disapproved of there were four or five other parts of the venue people could go to. When a band had that problem we called them Freddie and the Snack Bar Fillers.

Manfred Mann's Earth Band entered that category. He'd binned all the pop stuff and was doing more 'out there' stuff and I said to Manfred, 'This is a dance hall – people are here to dance.' He told me, 'Don't worry man, I've been in this business a long time. Let me tell you how we start the show: there's an air-raid siren, the lights come up, I'm wearing this rainbow jacket and I go straight into 'There'll Always Be An England'. I said, 'If you do that, there won't be an Earth Band!'

Everyone's expecting '5-4-3-2-1' and all that. Tiger Tim had a record cued, I had my hand on the plugs that powered the sound system, Manfred went: 'There'll always be an—' and I pulled the plug. Right away Tim said: 'Manfred seems to be having technical problems. We'll get him back soon!' and played the record. Manfred got his money and left. He never played.

Bands moving from pop to heavy rock or psychedelia was something a lot of the bookers didn't understand. The Sweet did it too. They went underground and a lot of people were caught out because they didn't realise their audience wouldn't like it.

Our success with the Electric Garden was to pay dividends for everyone who enjoyed live music in Scotland. The place was so successful that Frank Lynch's Unicorn Leisure began running the Playhouse Ballroom at the top of Green's Playhouse as Clouds. That did so well that we would eventually take over the entire Playhouse, which would become the Glasgow Apollo. That came about because of the enthusiasm people had for what we were offering.

COLIN ROBERTSON: I have a favourite story which explains most people's attitude to the dancin' ... There's a well-known character in Glasgow called Archie who started as a bank robber. He described himself as 'in the banking business – withdrawals only'. He escaped from Barlinnie once ... and was recaptured in the Locarno while he was giving it some moves. He told me later he hadn't realised he was the only one dancing as the police moved in.

Another night he saw a girl in the queue for the Locarno and he fell in love right away. Inside he saw her dancing with her pals, plucked up the courage and asked for a dance. She said: 'Yes.' So later that night he asked to walk her home. She said: 'No.' He asked to walk her to the bus. She said: 'No'. He asked whether he could see her again. She said: 'Maybe.'

So the weeks go by and he's getting closer – he's allowed to hold her hand and stuff. He realises he's got the stamp of approval when she says one night: 'Would you like to meet Albert?' He knows that's the sign that he's in – but he doesn't know why!

So it's arranged, and he gets himself dolled up and goes to her place to meet Albert. He's brought into the house and meets the sister, the mother and father, has a cup of tea and all that.

Eventually she says: 'Are you ready to meet Albert?' He says: 'Oh yes ...' and by now he's only thinking about one thing. So she leads him down the hall and takes him into a bedroom. Propped up on the bed is a really old guy: he's the grandfather, Albert. He's got a napkin tucked in and one of the sisters is feeding him soup from a bowl.

They both look round as the door opens – and the sister misses Albert's mouth with the spoon and the hot soup burns his chest. Albert screams out in pain and our man Archie bursts out laughing. The whole family appear and they're totally horrified: 'You laughed at Albert!' And they attack him – the whole family! He ends up bolting with a stab to his bum which ruined his mohair suit. And he never did get what he was after.

Trying harder: Tear Gas after moving on from the Bo Weavles era, above; and Dave Batchelor with his boy-band days behind him, far right.

The Glasgow Apollo, right, was to become a legendary venue

The Shadettes embraced 'head music' and become heavy rockers Nazareth, still featuring Pete Agnew, left

11 He was a big star ... but he went too far with the chicken stunt

WHEN Unicorn gave up the lease on the Electric Garden in 1971, it closed on a Sunday – and Clouds was to open at the top of the Playhouse on the Friday. It was a challenging week. But the new venue turned out to be a great success from the start.

We also ran the Cavendish in Edinburgh as another Clouds. It's a fantastic hall and has that special feel that only a few places have. It has a few rooms and those rooms have hosted every band imaginable from the big band era to people like Slade. The requirement was you had to be drunk. Like a lot of these places you didn't need more than one jacket to be a regular – there weren't many mirrors and you could dance by stepping from one leg to the other.

GEORGE WALLACE: I grew up in Cheshire when most people were getting into the Beatles and the Stones, but that wasn't for me. I was listening to the soul music coming out of the States like the Four Tops, the Temptations and so on.

My sister got me into northern soul. When I was home on leave from the navy she'd be full of stories about all-nighters. She'd play one single on repeat for hours at a time – happy days!

In 1972 I was posted to HMS Nubian at Rosyth. Not long afterwards I met Maureen, who'd been to some of the northern soul nights down south. The rest is history – we got married two years later.

But it was hard to get much soul music of any kind played anywhere. I even used to take records with me when I went out to clubs. That's what happened at the Angus Hotel in Dundee when I was asked to DJ since I'd been supplying records. Soon I was DJing every Sunday night, and later I did some all-nighters in the Marryat Hall and there were great things happening in Clouds and Tiffany's in Edinburgh.

GORDON GURVAN: I started going to the Palais in Dundee in the 1970s when they used to have an under 18 disco on Sunday evenings. It was a disco with band on stage too – but looking back, it's the strange custom I remember most. As the dancefloor filled up everyone would start walking around the edge in a big circle, around and around all night. It was the guys eyeing up the talent – when you fancied nipping in for a jig, you'd leave the revolving mass, have your wee dance, then go back and join the revolving mass again! I thought it was a bit weird ...

The fashion around that period was high-waistband trousers with 12 buttons, wedge-soled shoes and a velvet jacket. It sounds a bit 'Man at C&A' now!

MOIRA WILSON: Tiger Tim was great – he really was a big star as far as we were concerned, and good-looking as well. But he went too far when he did the chicken stunt in Cumnock Town Hall. It was just about the time Alice Cooper had killed a chicken on stage, so Tim dressed up as Alice and did a similar thing.

The chicken was already dead, and plucked and everything, but Tim ran onto the stage with a top hat on and a big knife, and started cutting it to bits and throwing bits into the crowd. I'd seen some trouble in the town hall before – we all had – but this was mental. A lot of us, me included, worked for Marshall's Chunky Chicken, so the way we saw it, he was taking the mickey out of our jobs. I don't think the Alice Cooper connection came across as much as the idea he was laughing at us. It's funny now, of course!

The police had been called when Tim pulled the stunt in Glasgow, so it wasn't that much of a surprise to have the Cumnock version turn up as well. It *was* a surprise to see our DJ arrested though – he spent a night in the cells for being in possession of a knife, which was the best thing they could do him for.

GORDON NICOL: Iron Virgin had quite a different dynamic from any other band I'd been in. We were an image-conscious lot – Stuart Harper, the singer, was quite the seamstress and made me a few jumpsuits along with his own. My favourite was like a jester suit: purple polka dots on white for one side and white polka dots on purple for the other side. With my 6-inch platform boots in blue and silver it was quite a striking outfit.

We only played Clouds in Glasgow once but it was great and had everything going for it – a really amazing atmosphere and tons of people thronging the dance floor. But we were banned after our gig ... At the time we opened our act with ELO's 'Roll Over Beethoven'. All three guitarists would be seated while Stuart, in tux and tails, would conduct us through the intro. Just when it went into the Chuck Berry guitar riff, Stuart would rip off the tails and reveal a gold lamé jumpsuit replete with chastity belt, No Entry sign and padlocks.

It was always a real showstopper – and because of that we'd been told before going on that if we did the song that way, we wouldn't be back. But we did do it that way, and sure enough the crowd stopped dancing and stood gaping at us, struck by the absolute theatre of it all.

The management at Clouds wanted the crowd to be dancing the whole time – they must have felt that if they stopped, they didn't like it or something. So we were banned and never got to go back. But it was worth it and the crowd lapped it up big-time.

Attitudes were changing in Clouds and Colin Robertson decided to move on. He went back to what had been the Electric Garden and opened it as Shuffles, and very quickly began to do well. He was in direct competition with Clouds, which we were promoting very hard. We brought in the Bay City Rollers, the Glitter Band and a host of hit artists of the time. We filled it every week – it was over-capacity so you couldn't get everyone in who wanted in.

All those disappointed punters went to Shuffles. We were paying for the bands to play but Colin was filling Shuffles with the people who couldn't pay us to see the bands. One night with the Bay City Rollers I had to leave the building, go round the back and up the fire escape just to get backstage – and Shuffles was full that night on the back of us.

COLIN ROBERTSON: I wasn't concerned that Unicorn could outspend us – in fact I was betting on it. I wanted them to spend money on aspects of the business that I considered had a lower priority. I read a book called *Painting Walls With Light* which convinced me that projecting lights onto walls gave us tremendous variation in decor, just by changing the lighting effects around each week or so.

So while Clouds would have to spend lots of money on one wall covering, it looked as if we were redecorating every week. That made customers happy with us – they felt we cared for them enough to keep redecorating.

Shuffles had five separate areas linked together, and we could open each part as the crowd grew in number. This gave the the impression that we were always busy and that ensured a good atmosphere. One secluded area was called 'Cuddles Corner' and it was well named.

Meanwhile, the city of Glasgow entered one of its most violent phases in terms of the dancin'. There had been a number of muggings in Sauchiehall Street in the 1970s and the police had put a plain-clothes cop in the street, who had to pretend to be drunk all day. He had to pretend to stagger about all day and all night and they'd given him a bag with sausages in it for realism, and a brick underneath them.

So you'd have gangs coming down to the door and threatening to kill you, as they did every week, and in those days there was no CCTV and no radios, so the police weren't coming unless they were already there.

But the undercover cop would go up to the gang outside, and he'd say, 'Those bastards in the club are asking for it, let's get them …' and he'd lead a charge, letting the guys get in front of him as they approached the door. We'd open it, ready for them, so they'd start to back off – but he'd force them on, stopping them from backing out until he'd pushed them in the door where our bouncers dealt with them.

We had two bad characters who threatened to kill everybody, tried to assault everybody, and you had to break them. So this plain-clothes cop was in the club with us, and he pulls out a knife and says to one of these guys, 'I'm going to slash you – which side of your face do you want it on?' The guy's like, 'Yeah, right,' but the cop kept at it up until the guy broke – he burst into tears and said: 'The right hand side please!' It was harsh but you *had* to break them – the alternative was innocent people getting hurt. You kept the peace by being badder than the bad guys. You *had* to win the fight.

COLIN ROBERTSON: One night two officers came into Shuffles and just stood there at the edge of the dance floor. They were completely killing the atmosphere – until one of them took off his hat and dropkicked it into the crowd. They were totally drunk! There was a lot of that went on. It's a well-known fact that the reason so many coppers die soon after they retire is they discover the real price of drink …

A friend of mine was once about to be done for drunk driving, but the two officers told him: 'You're in luck because we're too drunk to do you – so we'll put your keys in the exhaust pipe, take you to the station and bring you back when our shift finishes.'

And a guy who's quite high up now once hung out of a back window in Shuffles on a rope because he didn't want the visiting sergeant to realise how drunk he was.

One unforgettable night the Bo Weavles had played the Flamingo in Glasgow's Paisley Road West when the venue was closed. They were half-way through 'This Old Heart of Mine', the national anthem at the time, when a guy kicked off. The big steward had him very quickly and started squeezing his head, so I thought he was winning. But the guy shouted 'Govan! Govan!' the war-cry of his gang – and right away a table came over the balcony and the whole place disintegrated. *Everybody* got assaulted. The band kept playing 'This Old Heart of Mine' for about 20 minutes and the fight just would not stop …

It's amazing how it had started as well. George, our singer, was a very good-looking guy so he was getting a lot of attention from the girls. The gang leader was a bit unhappy about that so he'd gone down the front to tell him: 'You're gettin' it.' But George, who was a nice guy, just thought it was a request for a song, and couldn't hear what was being said so asked him to

The Toddy Bowl Bar in the Strathpeffer Pavilion

speak up. That was a red rag to a bull – the guy on the floor started shouting the odds and that's when the bouncer had jumped in.

DAVE BATCHELOR: There was a police station across the road so the police came in mob-handed. They closed the road in both directions and dozens of people were jailed. There were batons in the hall. People were trying to free other people who'd been arrested. The police station was full and people were trying to break in, so a police van was loaded up, taking people to another jail – and it got ten yards before it was overturned.

ARTHUR SCOTT: My favourite Strath story relates to a young woman from the Ferry in Inverness who was having a 'quiet drink' with her friends in the Toddy Bowl bar when she was accosted by an acquaintance, who started a heated argument. Feeling threatened and trying to defend herself, in one fluid gunslinger move she loosened one of her white stilettos, flicked it up with her toe, caught the front in her hand and brought the heel down on her assailant's scalp, causing a great deal of blood to be spilt.

Needless to say she didn't get the value of her ticket that night, quickly finding herself three hours early for her bus home. She was not the only

Slade were a massive band in Scotland – here Noddy Holder demonstrates stair usage for the Sleaz Band

one – any fighting or aggressive behaviour resulted in a swift ejection through the emergency door in the men's toilets.

DEREK L: We only fought other gangs – we dealt with business ourselves and didn't bring other people into it, and that's the way we kept things. One of my lot got stabbed one night in a hall on the southside of Glasgow. They had him in a room while they waited for the ambulance and he heard the manager saying how much bother it was going to cause the hall. My mate said: 'Here's the deal – if you let me go I'll say I was stabbed in the Savoy!' So they let him go and when he got to hospital himself that's what he told the police. It's another example of keeping other people out of the business.

CHRIS F: A lot of places had a trick they used to keep the blame from their doors. If you wound up becoming unconscious in a club, for whatever reason, you'd find yourself waking up in a back street outside the club – with tickets for another club in your pocket. Then when the police asked you what happened you'd say you fell over, and when they search you they'd find those tickets so they wouldn't think there'd been any bother in the club you'd actually been in.

But despite the downsides, that venue at 480 Sauchiehall Street was always a magical place. Colin moved on and I was sharing an office with him at the time so I renamed Shuffles as the Mayfair, introduced an alcohol license and ran it like that for about three years.

That license actually made our ability to fill the place much harder. When Slade had played there during its Electric Garden era you could get 1300 to 1500 people in. Once it was licensed you had age restrictions. But no one complained about the ages of the crowd until then.

The Mayfair also introduced Glasgow to one of the dance hall scene's most memorable characters, Jet Mayfair. Mayfair after the club and Jet because he could move on the dance floor. He very soon became a mascot for the scene and the business, and when you have a character like him around you should celebrate it. Depending on when you talk to him he's been a secret agent, a political motivator or just a wee guy working on the railroad.

Visiting stars like Johnny Cash and Carl Palmer were either delighted or shocked by him. Noddy Holder loved him to bits and he jammed with Slade – and many others – on our stages every time we turned our backs. He nearly got shot when he hid in a cupboard to meet Diana Ross and he nearly got us shot when he took the mic and told a hall full of Christian mums and nuns: 'Kick out the jams you motherfuckers!' There could be a book about Jet Mayfair. I hope one day there will be.

Slade were without doubt our biggest regular draw. Status Quo were huge – those two were the biggest acts in Scotland.

COLIN ROBERTSON: Slade were always nice guys. Easy to work with, never a problem, and stuck to their word. They made a tremendous difference to us because they stayed with us after they'd made it big, which made us look important.

That building is probably the best venue ever in Scotland. I say that because of the number of brilliant artists who cut their teeth there and got the best out of it: David Bowie, Pink Floyd, the Sensational Alex Harvey Band, Supertramp, H2O, Midge Ure, the Average White Band, Orange Juice – I could go on. So many huge bands played there before they made it and we were all blessed to be a part of that.

I'll never forget the time Marc Bolan drew himself a circle in the middle of the stage and sat down to perform, but he was so far back the audience couldn't see him. We asked him to move forward a bit with his circle. He said 'no'. We asked him why he was sitting down to play. He told us to run along. So the crowd saw the top of his head while he warbled 'Ride A White Swan'. What a memory!

It's had a great history and it continues to do brilliantly as the Garage. As long as it's run by someone who understands how good it is, it'll always do well.

COLIN ROBERTSON: It was common for enterprising people in towns like Saltcoats, Lanark and so on to organise buses to take people from their area into Glasgow for a night's dancing. We actively sought out potential organisers and offered them an incentive like 10% of the door money they brought to us. The punters would dance the night away and then meet the bus for the journey home. Add alcohol to the scenario described and things were bound to happen.

One evening a popular steward took a fancy to one of the out-of-towners. They arranged a quick kiss and cuddle at the end of the night and of course the young lady missed the bus back to Saltcoats. The young sir had a works van and took her home ... eventually. She became pregnant and love ensued. They got married, had two other children, are still happily together today in Troon. Romance by chance!

Iron Virgin have the sound of Eastern promise

PORTOBELLO, sometimes laughingly referred to as the Brighton of the East, is famous for its swimming pool, beach and power station.

You can now add to that list a pop group . . . IRON VIRGIN.

And although it might sound incongruous the five-strong Iron Virgin are about to give birth to a hit, a song called "Rebels

This page: Iron Virgin demonstrate the look which got them into trouble in Glasgow

Opposite: Tiger Tim demonstrates the act which got him arrested in Cumnock Town Hall

12 There was a guy with a wooden leg – half his moves were good

THE YEARS between the 1940s and the early 1970s saw regular changes to the dance hall scene. Many types of music, types of dance and types of venues flourished then died as progress kept moving forward. But by the mid-70s the pace of change was markedly faster – and the next wave of progress would leave the dancin' in a position which looked like the beginning of the end. And in a way, it was.

Technology played a big part in all of that. Sound systems began to become more complex and started sounding much better. But the result was the death of bands in clubs, because you couldn't make a band sound the way new records did. People were beginning to travel further afield on their holidays too, and could see extravagant lifestyles on the telly like never before.

COLIN ROBERTSON: There was a change of mood. People from outside the business took a look at what was going on and came in with the notion that what was needed were big flash lavish places like the ones they'd seen in London. They didn't work – but they did a lot of damage to what had been there previously. People didn't want the new thing but they didn't want to go back to the old thing either.

The thing that had worked was the expensive new sound systems. People started bolting bass bins to the floor and getting that thump. But the sound system in the Mayfair came from old speakers hanging on the walls – I had better speakers in my house than the ones in the club.

The next problem was that the new sound systems showed up the old records to be dull and flat. Boney M's early stuff is a great example – they had a German sound with a big strong bass and everything was clear. That kind of music sounded much better than all the records we'd been playing for years.

Some styles of music on record sounded better than others. A good example is northern soul, which caused a headache because Glasgow didn't get into it. But a good proportion of the punters, and good punters at that, used to hire buses and go down to Wigan Casino. Five buses going to Wigan was five busloads who weren't coming into one of our clubs. That's the first time I realised what some of the operators in Saltcoats or wherever must feel when people took buses into the city centre.

PAUL MASSEY: Northern soul became an east coast phenomenon in Scotland – hundreds of dancers would fill venues like Aberdeen Music Hall, Clouds in Edinburgh and the Marryat in Dundee. But it didn't sit comfortably with what I would consider the traditional concept of the dancehall. The music was the main appeal of the scene. People went specifically to listen and dance to it. You didn't go for general socialising. It had its own fragile etiquette and traditions and if the scene was diluted in any way then a lot of its appeal would go too.

LINDSAY HUTTON: The Leapark Hotel in Grangemouth was the scene where we'd take punk records and get the DJ to play them. It was always practically deserted and we'd buy shirts from the charity shops and spray bullet holes on them like the Heartbreakers. This was in the day when you got a supper thrown in with the entry fee, usually pie and beans or something exotic like that.

The International Hotel in Grangemouth was part of a circuit at one time. Brian Guthrie was the promoter there and he had Echo and the Bunnymen, U2, the Associates and Marillion there amongst many others. The Rezillos' early shows were a revelation and made it seem like a little bit of CBGB's was available locally. The Dream Boys played there, featuring Peter Capaldi and Craig Ferguson with Roddy Murray and Temple Clark. They were very vaudevillian and covered Iggy's The Passenger long before most people cared about the punk rock Ozzy. Roddy can be seen in *Local Hero* as one of The Ace-Tones and now runs the An Lanntair arts centre in Stornoway.

Brian and I put on some shows at Grangemouth Town Hall. We had the Rezillos, Simple Minds and Ultravox among others. It was a great venue. Brian put on a show with Squeeze where Simple Minds opened for them. Squeeze had just had a hit with 'Take Me I'm Yours' and got somewhere in the region of 90 people. Anyway, the first A & R person from London to see Simple Minds came to that show. It was Howard Thompson from Bronze Records. It was pretty exciting because I knew he'd signed Eddie and the Hot Rods. I think he might have tried to do something with the band if he hadn't been about to leave Bronze for CBS. The little red star badge that Jim Kerr wears on the back sleeve of *Life In A Day* was given to him by Howard.

There were so many different forms of music and so many different forms of dance. Along with the most popular moves of the day, the Mayfair and the Venue downstairs served audiences who wanted to pogo to the emerging punk bands, jive to jazz to line-dance to country and western. Andy Daisley ran a lot of those jazz and country nights – at the latter he'd even hold fast-draw competitions and people would turn up in full cowboy, Red Indian or US Cavalry outfits. They called themselves things like Wild Bill and Cavalry Joe, and had a great time. Tommy Samson's Big Band was still playing to people who wanted ballroom dancing and you could also enjoy roller-disco at the Mayfair and in the Penthouse above the Apollo.

DEBORAH FOY: At seventeen and a half years of age I was terrified I'd have to deal with the embarrassment of not getting into Bentley's in Kirkcaldy. My friend and I slowly went up the stairs and the bouncers looked at us – and said, 'Evening, ladies.' That was it: Bentley's nearly every night of the week!

Everyone got dressed up to go dancing. There was none of the jeans and T-shirt brigade – it was guys in suits with big baggy trousers that puffed up when they were spinning round. And there was the new romantic phase when the guys wore more make-up than us! Everyone danced in those days and not the step-together type of dancing they do today.

There were always buses coming in from the west. One night a guy in a white suit was ushered out and said he was going to come back and kill the bouncers, who just turned away. A short while later he did come back and soon he was rolling about in the foyer with one of the bouncers. All of a sudden a huge stink came up – the guy had soiled himself, and in a white suit as well! After that he was quickly ejected, but all I kept thinking about was those poor folk who would be on the bus home with him. That would have felt like a long journey ...

LINDSAY HUTTON: A guy called Bob Sutherland started putting on punk/new wave shows at The Maniqui in Falkirk. It was a pretty good set up because you'd get a London band with a local combo opening. It gave the likes of Johnny and the Self Abusers the chance to trounce the competition. Anyway, it came to pass that the Stranglers came to town. I'd written a negative review or something about the show they played at Glasgow City Halls and bassist JJ Burnel wanted me to be ejected from the venue or they wouldn't play. A petty display of exactly why I hated them then, and actively dislike them to this day. Long story short, I wasn't escorted off the premises and stayed for two songs before leaving of my own volition because they stank. Maniqui was a good place but the central region has always had a problem with supporting live music. I think Bob had to give it up because he lost money more often than not.

GORDON GURVAN: The old Palais in Dundee turned into Samantha's. Its main entrance was in South Tay Street, but you could also get in via the Stage Door pub round the back in the Marketgait. There was a cage in the centre where they had go-go dancers and the DJ was Sandy Martin. They had the occasional band too but the place didn't last very long – it was remodelled into Bloomers after about eighteen months.

By this time, Billy Connolly was a very big name and had come a long way since we managed him as a folk musician. But even though he didn't do that any more, his influence had been strong in changing the folk club scene. Billy had done well in those wee clubs but as he got bigger it was our job to make more money for him. I'd say to the guy who ran a club: 'Why don't you increase your fee?' He'd say, 'We can't – we've only got a capacity of 100 people.' I'd say, 'Get a 500 then.' He'd say, 'We can't – this is the folk club and we're not moving.' Oh well, I'd do it then – I'd hire a big hall and fill it from the folk club. And so ended the folk clubs and Billy Connolly.

Glasgow's Savoy became a big success in the 1970s. Everyone knew what it was all about. The music, the drink, and everything was made to make it easy to meet and enjoy people's company. No mirrors so you don't see yourself, dislike your appearance and want to go home. Fast bar service so you can get as much drink as you like. Low lighting so you can't make out what people look like. A nice haze, plus music with a steady beat so people who can't dance can at least move from side to side and enjoy it. So there's a right good chance you'll get off with each other. The Savoy was like the perfect storm for that.

> **COLIN PATON:** A line that worked for me in the Savoy – we used to call it the 'Sav-swav' – was: 'Here doll, do you mind if I ask you something? Do you believe in the hereafter? Aye? That's brilliant because I'm here after a lumber ...'

Things were changing in all directions, but there was life in the dancin' yet, and the great thing was that no matter what kind of night you wanted to find, you could find it somewhere. That was true outside the cities, in places like Ayr, Dundee, the Borders, Cumnock and Arran which were all bouncing with life.

> **TIGER TIM STEVENS:** I was DJing at the Lamlash Halls on Arran. Charlie Currie announced me with the usual big build-up, but I was asleep under the table in the dressing room. By the time they woke me up I was sober enough to do the set, but my security man Donnie Cowden gubbed someone in the crowd who'd been bad-mouthing me. I gave him hell for it, and he went off in a mood. We found him next morning lying on the beach, where he'd fallen over a wall drunk. I couldn't really say anything because I hadn't set a good example myself.

I judged a Miss Arran contest at the Lamlash Halls – but there wasn't any judging involved. She'd been chosen in advance because she'd agreed to spend the prize money on drink. I was so drunk I couldn't tell the difference between contestants and had to be told which one to vote for. I don't remember what she looked like but I do remember she bought a lot of drink.

One time we took the Sleaz Band there with Slade. The Sleaz Band used to fight each other in the dressing room and go on with bleeding noses and stuff. They were always exceptionally drunk as well. One time in Arran the bass player collapsed down the stage stairs as he went on, and could not be woken up. Noddy Holder from Slade went on, grabbed the bass and played the set with the rest of the band.

COLIN ROBERTSON: We had a band called the Dead End Kids and because Eddie and I knew Tam Paton we'd been able to get them on tour with the Bay City Rollers, so they were hot at the time. I got a call from the label asking where they were playing on a certain night, because there was a party of Japanese people who wanted to video them. Unfortunately they were playing Cumnock Town Hall on the night in question.

So I hired a couple of limousines and we took these Japanese guys to see Electric Brae and Burns Cottage and all that. Then the dreaded Cumnock Town Hall ... We arrived in these limousines and we got out to see two guys sitting on the steps covered with blood. They'd been put out for battering each other, but at Cumnock you only got put out until you'd sobered up, then you got back in.

We took them past that and into the hall, and the place was jumping. The band got on stage and right away the riot started. Robbie, the singer, had to hit a guy with a mic stand in the first minute – it was mayhem. The Japanese guys had lost all interest in the band and were photographing the fight. We took them to a restaurant later and they were still talking about the fight, and not a word about the Dead End Kids.

Jock McCurdie would stagger on stage pished and interrupt the bands to announce, 'The buses are leaving for Drongan, Auchinleck ...' One night when Tear Gas were playing he came out, missed the mic, and clattered onto the hall floor. So Davie the singer interrupted his own song and said: 'The buses are leaving for Drongan, Auchinleck ...'

Back in the 1960s I'd booked Desmond Dekker and the Aces into Auchinleck, which had a lot of bands in those days. No one had ever seen a black man in Auchinleck, never mind heard reggae music. So the curtains opened and Desmond started singing Israelites to complete and utter silence. The audience had never seen or heard anything like it, and they were asking: 'What is that?' I told them, 'It's the number one single this week.' Someone said: 'Not in Auchinleck!'

COLIN ROBERTSON: There's a cartoon from 40 years ago which shows a peacock strutting his stuff, all done up and arrogant, and a female bird saying, 'That's all very well, but how good are you in bed?' That's really the attitude in the dancin' throughout its time.

I know of quite a few long-term relationships that started in Shuffles, and not just among the punters. I recently went to the 40th wedding anniversary of a couple who met there. One of the stewards, Tam Teeth, and a barmaid, Patricia, got together at work. They got married and remained working in Sauchiehall Street by which time Tam was venue manager and Patricia was bar manageress. It wasn't only customers who fell in love in the intoxicating atmosphere of the disco.

For some girls, of course, the allure of the business was not so easily dealt with. Many girls, both staff and punters, bcame pregnant and remain single mums to this day. The fathers ranged from customers to band members and roadies.

Cheeky Easdale's interpretation of the cartoon that so aptly encapsulates the spirit of the dancin'

One time I was asked by a lady who was previously a go-go dancer with us if she could hire the function suite for her son's 18th birthday. I let her have it for free – we'd remained friends over the years. I met her son on the big night and he was a really nice young man. Much later in the evening after many drinks, he came up to me and quietly asked me: 'I don't suppose you could possibly be my dad, could you?' I assured him I wasn't, but if I had been I'd be very proud of the way he'd turned out.

KEVIN DONNELLY: I was at university in Aberdeen and I shared a flat with this force of nature called Ricky. He really believed in himself, which was amazing because he wasn't half the man he thought he was! One night we were in the dancin' and he spotted this group of three girls and told us: 'I'm going home with them – all of them.' We just thought, yeah, of course you are.

But after we'd left and gone for fish and chips, the same three girls were in the queue in front of us. They got served and left, and Ricky said: 'Sorry guys, I've got to bin you – I'm away with them.' And he left the shop and followed them. Little did he know we followed him out and stood on the corner. They went to get into a car and Ricky went up, opened the fourth door and said: 'Going my way, girls?' The driver didn't pause for a second – she told him where to go in two words.

By the time he turned round we were back in the chip shop, and acted amazed when Ricky came back in. We asked him what had happened and he said, 'Guys, I just couldn't do it to you – what kind of a night would you have without me?'

DONALD DOYLE: There was a guy with a wooden leg who used to come to the dancin' in Inverness every weekend without fail. I'm not kidding, but exactly half his moves were good and half his moves were bad! Every now and again someone would stand on his false foot, and he'd fall over, making sure the wooden leg bent round at a terrible angle, then scream in agony for a laugh. Bouncers all over the place kept telling him to stop it and I think he got barred from most halls because he wouldn't – it really was funny though.

The John Travolta movies were a revolution for the dancin'. In 1978 *Saturday Night Fever* defined dancing for a generation, exactly the way the twist had done in 1960. And it was great for the halls – because for the first time in years people were queuing down the street to get in.

It was incredible. But it was obvious – after years of hearing music you couldn't dance to, the general public was hearing strict-tempo stuff you could very easily move about to. Everyone could do it, and everyone wanted to. As a result of more money coming in, we could all afford to put those sound systems in. I remember being astonished at some of the systems – 20,000 watts in a club! But it was clean sound: you could hear everything. The sound in the room was as good as the producer had made it in the studio. That was the key thing that made the disco era such a success – along with the tunes, of course.

KEVIN DONNELLY: John Travolta, 'Stayin' Alive', 'Disco Inferno' – what's not to love? I went to see it in Glasgow with my girlfriend, now my wife, and as soon as it was finished we decided to go up the dancin'. It seemed like half the crowd from the showing had the same idea. It was years since I'd queued to get into a dance hall. It was like a rebirth – we had years of great times ahead.

STEVIE TAYLOR: I met a stunning girl in the Mayfair after being inspired to hit the town after seeing *Saturday Night Fever*. She was the best-looking girl in the place – sitting in an area off the main hall, she seemed to be spending the night fending off men. But after a few drinks I managed to sit down near her. That's as close as I thought I'd get.

A guy came up to her and said something like: 'Can you tell me how come you're so beautiful?' She said: 'I must have got your share!' The guy went away, defeated, but I was killing myself laughing.

Another guy came up and went: 'Is anyone sitting here?' She said: 'No.' But as he sat down he made it obvious he was going to lean straight into her so she said: 'Are you stupid? I told you no one was sitting here!' He went away, and I was laughing again.

That went on with different guys for about 15 minutes, but she knew she had me as a kind of audience. By that time we were both laughing at her killer lines. She asked me to come over and I said: 'You'll be pleased to hear I don't have any chat-up lines.' She said: 'But you've had all those hints!' We had a great night and wound up getting married four years later.

1980s~2000s

As forms of entertainment cycle
and renew themselves, will the
future of the dancin' turn out
to be embedded in its past?

THE MORE THINGS CHANGE

13 How does it feel to come to the dancin' with your daughter?

THE 1980s were an exciting time for me – as they were for a new generation of dancers. I spent much of the decade working for Stakis as they developed their clubs all over Scotland. I was privileged to enjoy great relationships with a lot of different communities all over the country. But underneath it all there was a search going on to identify the next big thing. What was it going to be? When I found it, it wasn't what I'd expected – but it *did* turn out to be big. In the meantime, of course, the dancin' remained about what it had always been about.

STU WHO?: I was in a very snobby venue in Edinburgh when I noticed a very attractive young lady enter the room. Her long auburn hair had that deep-red Celtic sheen and a loosely curled flow, like a maiden in a Renaissance painting. Well tasty!

From over my shoulder I heard a male voice starting a chat-up line – in a pseudo-Sean Connery, deep-toned Scottish accent he went: 'Well, hi there! Is your hair naturally that curly? Or is it just the shape of your *heid*?'

Yeah, 'heid' – his attempt at a posh accent had broken down on the very last word. I tapped him on the shoulder, gave him my business card, and said: 'No offence, but if you ever get a lumber with patter like that, could you give me a wee call? Because if you do, there's hope for us all ...'

AUDREY MILNE: Sometimes the best lines were just for a laugh – there wasn't any plan to make a move after the guy had said it. Like being asked for a dance and you'd say, 'Aye, I'm dancin',' and he'd say: 'Thanks – I wanted the seat.' If someone asked you: 'Where have you been all my life?' you'd answer: 'By the look of you I wasn't alive for most of it.'

ELAYNE LOW: When I started going to the dancin' in Edinburgh I was wearing the dodgy fashions of the day like puffy skirts and tops with the little scarf attachments, court shoes and white boxy handbags. But I soon came to hate all of that, plus the Wham! T-shirts, white stilettos, streaked hair and all that. It looked naff and cheap – and besides, I liked black.

I didn't like the chrome and mirror meat-markets either – I started going to dark dingy places and began getting into obscure bands and darker music. I became a 'goth' type as my musical taste widened and I got into wearing stringy mohair jumpers, home-made tartan miniskirts, black buckle boots and leggings. My prize possession was a black PVC skirt which cost me £6! I treasured it.

The hairstyle of the time was dyed black, crimped and teased out to fantastic proportions – all the clubs smelled heavily of hairspray. It was a nightmare if it rained. People would stand waiting outside clubs with plastic bags on their heads to protect their hairdos. The make-up for us was black eyeliner, pale foundation and either red or pale lipstick – a few wore black but I never suited it, although I had a funky pale blue lipstick, from a theatrical shop, which I loved. I used to borrow my dad's good tuxedo jacket and I was found out by the giveaway blue lipstick mark!

Getting ready to go out was a ritual with music on as your hair and make-up took ages to get right. You'd leave the house feeling great – only to come home piss-drunk, hair a mess and make-up like a panda.

GRAEME GRANT: Playing at Oil Can Harry's in Falkirk wasn't a good experience for me. They were pretty strict with us – you had exactly 20 minutes to set up at the start and exactly 20 minutes to get out at the end. My dad told me he'd been kicked out of the place when it was Doak's Ballroom in the 60s for getting too friendly with a girl, although it's not as if he had been up to much – just a wee kiss. But it was still owned by the Doak family in the shape of the grandson, Mr Johnston, so maybe strict rules was a family trait ... although you should have seen some of the behaviour at Oil Can Harry's on the cattlemarket nights.

ELAYNE LOW: We took lots of risks walking home in Edinburgh after the dancin' shut, taking dodgy shortcuts through closes and graveyards. Taxis were out of our price range and most of the time there were two or three people going the same way. Guys were gentlemen then, even punk and goth guys – they'd walk you home no problem.

One night around three in the morning my mate Fin and I decided to walk through the Canongate cemetery, telling ghost stories and trying to scare each other. Just as we went by an old crypt I saw a movement and heard a groan from the shadows – and set off screaming like the devil was after me. Fin went to investigate and found it was just an old tramp trying to get some sleep. He's never stopped bringing it up to this day.

Century 2000 in Edinburgh – because I ran it! – was one of the best halls ever ... It was an old picture hall and the busiest club in Edinburgh of its time. The manager, Martin Robb, was the best manager I ever worked with. There was a beautiful girl who worked there and she was always worth a laugh. Martin sent her to fill the company car with petrol and said: 'When you come back I'll give you the money for it'. So she drove the car to the garage, filled the tank, came back for the money, and then went back to the garage to pay!

Victoria's in Glasgow was opened by James Mortimer, almost exclusively to serve a guest list of James' friends. It quickly became a very busy over-25s club with an 18s club within it. For ten years or more it was the home of footballers, TV stars and anyone else who was anybody. James used his network of friends to build a VIP list that became the envy of everywhere else. It remained successful up until he sold it.

The Savoy went from strenth to strength. More children have been conceived in those fire exits than in any other club – and also, more people have received beatings in those same fire exits than in any other club. I was going to apply for a grant from the National Trust to have one of the fire exits walled with glass. Every hour, on the hour, two doormen would come out with someone and leather them, for people's enjoyment. The way a coal miner in a museum will show you how it used to be done – we'd have a historical re-enactment of someone getting pummelled then thrown down the stairs. It could become a community service sentence from the city courts ...

CATH McDONALD: My daughter was huge fan of H20, managed by Eddie, but she was only fourteen, so I asked Eddie if she could get in to see them at the Mayfair. Of course, he said she should just ask for him on the door and it would be fine. On the night, rather than let her and her pal go in themselves, I went with them to make sure they got in. The queue was right down the stairs but we walked up the other side to the door to be met by Eddie who shouted as loud as possible: 'How does it feel to come to the dancin' with your daughter?' He later told me that if he felt like Methusela I might as well feel bad as well ...

In Dunfermline the Kinema became Night Magic. Martin Robb and Alec were both GMs there at the time of Pete Waterman's Hitman and Her roadshows. It was a big big success in Dunfermline and brought in enormous money. That was a big roadshow and it was perfect for the Kinema because it was always a fun place.

Another club which played host to the Hitman show was Flicks in Brechin. Why should Brechin have a great night club? Well, it did. Flicks was opened by two guys called Mike and Stuart and became a Scottish institution when it was taken over by Ron Farquharson, who'd started as a steward, became its manager and eventually built an empire in America from his talents.

Flicks was rated in the top ten in the country. One of its centrepieces was an incredible light show including lasers, which they put on in the middle of the evening whenever they were open. Great music, great venue, great management. It really put Brechin on the map, and when it closed it took Brechin back off the map again.

AMANDA HAMILTON: They used to run free buses between Dundee and Brechin so you could go to Flicks. It was the best place in the area no question. The lights were incredible but the atmosphere was what made it. Twice I missed the bus back home and on both occasions the police helped me out – brilliant!

ROBBIE BLAIR: The light show was a ritual. Around 10.30 all the dancing would stop and the floor would clear for the lasers to start. The music was always the same: Star Trek, Star Wars, Superman and an exclusive mix of Patrick Cowley's Menergy. The club had drinks coasters which said 'Nicked from Flicks' on them – it worked ... you'd find them everywhere. A friend of mine had his bedroom door covered in them.

DAVE TAYLOR: The Hitman and Her night in Dunfermline was brilliant. Me and my three mates got right up the front and we're in the show for a good ten minutes. Of course, the clothes are a wee bit embarrassing now, but it's great to see the hair again!

DANNY GILLESPIE: I'm in a less well-known video ... One night I met a girl at the dancin' in Kirkcaldy and walked her home, but her parents had come home early. I didn't really want to take no for an answer but fortunately she didn't want me to either. So we found a nice wee bus shelter for cover. There were a group of young boys further up across the street but they weren't loud or anything so they didn't bother us. When we were heading home the boys gave us a round of applause, which we both took in the manner it was meant. I even waved – I'd had a great night!

About a month later a mate phoned me and told me there was a video doing the rounds of two people at it in a bus stop, and the guy looked like me. I thought it was funny till I took a moment to think. Sure enough – the wee guys down the road had had a video camera with them, and every move we made was available on VHS, right down to me waving at them after they'd cheered us! There wasn't much you could do but laugh. The annoying thing is, video cameras weren't small in those days so you'd think I might have noticed ...

Colin Robertson has always liked to pay attention to what the public might want next. He predicted the move into video and aimed to serve that market, so he opened the Videodrome

Scenes from Dundee: left,
Samantha's and the Barracuda;
this page, Da Vinci's and Sands

in Glasgow. There were neon lights and television screens everywhere – that took a lot of preparation, but Colin was committed to the task.

COLIN ROBERTSON: Kids were going about with Walkmans and the sound they were getting in their ears was incredible. It wasn't like listening to an old mono radio in an old Ford Anglia. People were buying high-performance decks and speakers. You had to compete with them. So I opened the Videodrome in Glasgow because video was going to be the next thing. The visual impact was tremendous and so was the sound.

The problem we've always had to fight over is public perception. That's why it's always important to prove to the audience you care about them. I'm not saying any of our ideas were original – I'm saying we used them well for our market.

But you always had problems with the licensing authorities. Eddie's spent years fighting them over the issue of plastic glasses. That's all about perception – how can it be right spending a fiver to get into a place then having to stand with a plastic glass? Even back in the day you couldn't do things like wet T-shirt competitions. The city council took a dim view of it and even if you did something like that on the QT you'd get a Sergeant Shinyshoes appearing saying, 'I heard you did a wet T-shirt contest the other week' ... Now of course there's really sleazy stuff going on and no one cares. I'm not saying it's right or it's wrong, but there was always that fight for perception.

Dundee people have been blessed with some great clubs. The two best things about Dundee are that it's always had a good dance hall, and it's the only place in Scotland you can buy a mince roll. It shows you they've got good taste!

At one point there was capacity for 8000 dancers within 200 feet, which was amazing for a town its size. De Stihls had been converted from an old jute warehouse and decorated as if it was a distillery.

Fat Sam's has been trading for nearly 30 years, and it's run fabulously by Angus Robb, and it's an example of how to make a night club popular. The Mardi Gras had been incredible. You wouldn't expect something that good outside the major cities, but it was that good under the management of Angus. The owners sold it on to a bigger company and the new owners didn't think things through – if they had, they'd have realised that Angus was the reason it was so good. But they didn't – so when he left and took over Fat Sam's he wiped out the Mardi Gras. He took it all the way to closure, which is very unusual.

GORDON GURVAN: De Stihls got into the 'acieed' movement in a big way. That was at the height of the rave scene, with acid house being a very intoxicating brew of dance beats and synth patterns. It wasn't just great music to dance to – it was also great to cycle to. I remember being out on my bike regularly during this era and would be plugged into my Walkman with acid pounding in my ears. It could be so mesmerising, a lot of times I ended up going much further than I'd planned without realising. I could have won the Tour de France on that stuff!

When I found the next big thing, it turned out to be Bonkers in Glasgow. I joined Daso Nicholas' company because I wanted to be next to the vision that created it. It was a stunning idea – Britain's first showbar. There were girls dancing on stage, competitions, over-25s rooms, dance-rooms, different bars on floors, things going on everywhere.

It was the busiest club in the city – every weekend night there were at least 2500 people in there. It was taking £100,000 a week when no other venue in Britain could dream of that.

The police called it 'the epicentre of all violence'. And without question it was the most violent hall I've ever known. It was closed for that reason – but what the police didn't know was it was the tip of an enormous iceberg.

On a weekly basis if there were less than ten serious assaults it would be astounding. When people were assaulted they were offered a blue t-shirt to replace their ruined clothes – but some people would say: 'I'm no' wearing a blue shirt, that's no' my team!' So the management started buying green ones too.

All the managers had medipacs on their belt, and when they got called to an incident they'd put on rubber gloves because they knew there would be blood. One night a guy was calling the manager by his name while he was being bandaged up: 'Thanks Jimmy, it's good of ye, Jimmy ...' The manager asked him, 'How do you know my name?' The guy said: 'You done me up last time I was bottled!'

They'd clean them up, give them a bag to put their bloodsoaked shirt in, and send them home with two tickets for the following week. That frightens people who live in Newton Mearns. But the reality is that if you come from a certain street, fighting isn't that bad. It hurts at the time but you get a free T-shirt and tickets for next week. Sometimes I think people would hit themselves to get the freebies!

I took the chairman of Scottish & Newcastle to see it. We went in and on that occasion there were 3000 in and he said: 'For God's sake, Eddie, get me out of here!' He was absolutely terrified. But the minute he left that night, the superpubs became part of S&N's strategy throughout Britain.

It was the beginning of the end of nightclubs, though – because Bonkers successfully mixed the dancin' with the pub. And the public loved it – it captured everybody's imagination.

The 1960s created entrepreneurial shows, where the show was what mattered. People had personality and events had spectacle. That went away to a great extent in the 1970s. But

Bonkers took that on and made lookalike acts very popular. At one point you had to sound like an act, then later it was more important to look like them. You had a lot of acts on that were nothing to do with music – but it's all Barnum and Bailey. It's all about the experience, and the dancers had a great time.

KENNY DUNCAN: I had a really lucky escape one night in Aberdeen when I'd just come off the rigs. I was having a pint waiting for the last train south when this real looker came into the pub and came right up to me. She had it all – and she knew what she wanted. She told me she had a hotel room nearby and she'd arrange for a flight to Glasgow for me in the morning, or a taxi if she couldn't get me a flight. She wasn't messing about.

You know that saying, if it's too good to be true it probably isn't true? I had a bad feeling about it so I decided to take it easy. About five minutes later a couple of guys came in and started calling over to her. She looked at me as if to say, 'It's your loss,' and went over to the other guys.

They left about ten minutes later and the barman came right up to me and said: 'That was a lucky escape.' Turns out she was the wife of a millionaire oil boss who couldn't afford to divorce her or something, but he had a private detective following her and everyone who went to a hotel with her wound up getting a kicking the next day.

WHY DON'T YOU
NITE CLUB

IN APRIL

upstairs at the playhouse - fri., sat., sun.

9 till late - the live disco - late bar

FRI **4** ANOTHER PRETTY FACE

PLUS TV 21

SAT **5** EVEREST AND The Delmonts

THE HARD WAY

FRI **11** JOSEPH K

AND Orange Juice & THE gobetweens

SAT **12** SKANITE

WITH TWO OF SCOTLAND'S BEST

THE RUDE BOYS + ALL THE RAGE

at last, the sound of
HEAVY METAL! THURSDAYS FROM APRIL 3RD

14 He always said his 'proper' dancing gladdened hearts

THE DEATHS of three people at the Hanger 13 rave in Ayr became a watershed moment in Scotland's dancin' history. No one came out of that situation looking good – but it was the clubs who paid most for that tragedy.

The Pavilion had a fine history as a ballroom. At one time the scene had been dominated by Bobby Jones' Ballroom until the arrival of Club de Mar in the late 1980s. Another Jones, Tom, was running the Pavilion as a rock venue. I ran Toledo Junction, a fabulous premises which is now Fury Murray's.

In the early 1990s the Pavilion began running its Hanger 13 rave nights. Rave music itself is no bad thing if that's what you want to hear, and there's no doubting it was very popular – but three deaths is sheer bloody negligence. It was probably a bad batch of eccies – also known as E, X, XTC, MDMA and so on – which killed three young people and send a number of others to hospital, but the events were much more far-reaching than that.

They closed the club. But despite what the police or the operators might say, it could have been prevented. Drugs were all too readily available in Hanger 13 and in the street outside. Everybody and their dog knew you could get E if you wanted it in the venue.

Most places don't even have one death. Three was such a big disaster that it helped force through a stack of new laws which clamped down on the dancin' trade – and the trade never recovered. The legislation wasn't needed. It was all common sense. Make sure people have access to water, make sure they don't have access to drugs, and a few more things which any club operator would know from day one.

COLIN ROBERTSON: Because everything was lumped in together, the business became associated with raving, which became associated with taking eccies. Which the vast majority of kids never did. That perception was wrong. It was perpatrated by the police, which was then taken on by the press. It just wasn't true, but the only people who were saying that was the operators, who'd already been tarred with the bad brush. We got hammered as being all baddies, when, as in most aspects of life, there were only a few baddies. Fortunately there were a lot of examples of good practice, even though some people might have been surprised to know about them. The Cathouse in Glasgow, the Ice Factory in Perth and a whole new movement in Aberdeen are great examples.

ALAN F: It's not worth arguing over the drugs debate – it's gone on forever and will continue. For some people it's part of the night out, for others it's criminal activity. but Hanger 13 was all about trying to be a club from the future, and for me it certainly was. People came from all over Scotland to be there and there were great nights with great music. It was unbelievable when they closed it, considering the amount of people who enjoyed it without any trouble. It hasn't really been equalled until maybe Fantazia at Braehead and the club scene has missed out on years of good times for that. So many nights are called 'Hanger 13 nights' because the original nights are remembered so well. We'd all go back – and all I'd say about the drugs issue is people don't go out to a club with the intention of not making it back.

DONALD MacLEOD: The Cathouse started as one night in Hollywood Boulevard on the Clydeside, the old Seaman's Institute. We just wanted a good night that we could enjoy, playing music we wanted to hear and meeting people we wanted to meet. It turned out everyone else did too – and that's how we ended up taking over the whole building.

It was brilliant but they always wanted rid of us, for reasons I could never understand. They kept trying to find reasons to cancel the lease. Once they got very close and we were making plans to close until our lawyer pointed out they hadn't given enough notice, so we could keep going. But I knew we'd never get an extension after that – especially after I'd given the owner the news that we were staying, and threw him down the stairs of his own venue!

So we spent a while looking for a new location and came up with Union Street, where we moved in 1995. For a last trick we tried to sell the old Cathouse building – even though it didn't belong to us ... and we'd have got away with it too if it hadn't been for the fact that the lawyer representing the prospective buyer also represented the real owner ...

It's also great having the Garage – it's an incredible place. We've had nights there which build on the history of what's gone before, like Prince playing. I love standing on the corner of the upstairs bar, because that's the place I used to pay the bouncers to let me take girls for a wee session when Eddie ran it as the Mayfair!

In Perth, John Bryden asked me to help him find a buyer for land in the city because he was thinking about a night club. He decided to build it himself and the Ice Factory became the best club in the area. He was fortunate to build it at the start of the acid era, where you had buses coming in from everywhere, and he was able to serve that market very well. He'd pack them in, sell them hamburgers which he was very proud of, and made enough money to send him to Spain, where he stayed until very recently.

I ran places in Aberdeen for seven years and never had one serious assault. It's a very nice city – although to get the most out of it you have to be from there.

Mr G's was owned by a guy called Ricky Simpson, who once owned Barneys. He lives in the Bahamas now, I understand. It's now called Tropicana but as Mr G's it really captured the market. Security was great, the music was great. Zig Zag ran for a time in direct competition to Mr G's, and did very well. I took it on it for a while but it didn't do anything for me and didn't do anything for the people of Aberdeen, so it closed.

Mike Wilson's triumph was to open a converted church – and call it the Ministry of Sin. At the time everybody objected – *everybody*! Opening a club with that name in a church suggested the devil was at work in Mike's brain. He fought long and hard to get it, and when he got it open it was hugely successful. He used the decor very well and it was a beautiful club. He still owns it now, and it's called the Pearl Lounge.

When the Tunnel opened in Glasgow Ron McCulloch was the driving force, under Colin Barr, one of the most creative operators in the city. It was novel, the sound system was sensational, it had fabulous DJs and the hall was perfect for that kind of dance music. Basements are perfect for dance music and it was a perfect basement. I think it's won more awards than any other club in Britain – and deservedly so. Colin started as a DJ in Toledo Junction in Paisley, and he's the first DJ I know who had a Porsche. Stakis bought it for him because it made the whole setup even better. Colin's tall and handsome with great taste ... the bastard.

FIONA BAILEY: The Volcano was made famous in 1996 as the venue in the club scene of *Trainspotting*. But my memories are more vivid of other nights in my home-from-home. An endless stream of the wannabe-cool watching the possibly cool, bobbing to mellow dance tracks, bottles of beer, furtive fumblings in the dark outshone by a few caught in flagrante on the banquettes. Another job for sweet short George the doorman. Kick everyone out, grab a few cases of beer which might be replaced some day, and head to Hyndland Road to find the usual suspects firing off walls full of pills, beer, jellies and dope.

One night the police visited to break up a casual game of road-tennis, only to have their radio nicked from the patrol car. Another night someone left a pile of human waste on the windowsill, complete with decorative crisps. We returned a frog to its devastated owner a week after it had been lost, although it was crushed and a little dry having spent time under cushions.

By seven in the morning there was no more beer but a friendly grocer at the end of the road would sell you Buckfast – even if you happened to be encased in toilet roll like a mummy. Home from home ...

KIRSTY ROBINSON: The first time I took an ecstasy pill was when I went to the Volcano. A friend of mine said he'd look after me so I felt quite confident – but soon after I'd taken it we went somewhere which had white brick walls, and I became convinced I was in prison. I don't know how I managed to get out of the toilet but I've never been so grateful to see my friend in my life.

LOUISE MADDEN: Me and a friend of mine, Katy, used to get in free to a few clubs in Dundee because we were bar staff. They still searched us because they had to, and this one night Katy realised she had a big lump of hash on her. We were already at the door so I had the bright idea of fumbling my pay packet, which you had to produce to prove you were bar staff, and scattering coins everywhere. It worked – the bouncers stopped to help me pick up my wages and forgot to search us. Another night a friend of ours, Bob, decided to act smart and get in free by pretending to be Mani from the Stone Roses. That worked too – and he did really look and sound like him.

Some of the chat-up lines were terrible. One guy asked me what my favourite sexual position was – I said anything that didn't involve him. Another one was: 'I dreamed about you last night' and the worst ever was: 'You remind me of my sister'. Yuck. But I couldn't believe it the night a guy came up to me and my friend and said: 'You'll be okay with me ladies – I've got a low sperm count!'

MARTIN DRUMMOND: We used to kill ourselves laughing with chat-up lines we'd never dare use, mainly because we were married by the time we thought of them. My favourite was: 'Hen, if I had a daughter you'd remind me of her!' closely followed by handing your target a set of keys and saying: 'Sorry, doll, I haven't had time to get a new set cut – take these for now and I'll be home when the pub shuts!' Up there with the classic: 'Have ye got 10p? Phone your maw and tell her ye'll not be home tonight ...'

BRIAN KANE: This would have been brilliant if I'd ever had the chance to use it ... You'd go up to a lassie, hold out your arm so your watch came out from under your jacket and wave it around in front of her, then look at it. She'd say: 'What are you up to?' and you'd reply: 'I'm trying out my new smart-watch.' She'd say, 'What's so smart about it?' and you'd tell her it was telepathic and it was telling you things about her. She'd want to know an example and you'd say: 'It says you don't have any underwear on.' She'd say: 'Well, it's not working, because I do have underwear on.' You'd look at the watch and go: 'Bloody hell, it's an hour fast!'

Signs of the times: Judging panel on Strictly Come Dancing, above; the Strath re-opened, right

ANDY CALDERWOOD: Best line I never used was to be reserved for a night that hadn't gone to plan: 'Sorry it didn't work out, hen – but do you have a sister?'

SHAUN H: Possibly my favourite memories from nights at the dancin' in the past few years are watching a midget and a six-foot tall transvestite argue, and watching a man dressed as a suicide bomber, when it wasn't Halloween, being questioned and charged under the Prevention of Terrorism Act ...

In my career I've been blessed to work in some of the best venues, with some of the best people, on some of the best nights Scotland has ever known. I can't believe that what started in Dave Batchelor's front room when I was 17 has taken me all round the world and given me so many laughs – so many I've only just scratched the surface here.

I have no doubt I've lived through a golden era on this planet. When it comes to the dancin' I'd say its golden era in Scotland was between the mid 70s and mid 80s. The music industry hadn't sorted itself into strict genres at that point and the dancin' was the beneficiary of all that. There were no rules so you got some great tunes – eternal tunes you could dance to for ever, from rock to pop to disco to new romantic and everything else.

In the mid-90s I opened four Babylons. I got Dave Batchelor in to take charge of the music

and we came up with a very sucessful formula. It had to have lyrics, so you could sing if you couldn't dance, or it had to be very danceable.

DAVE BATCHELOR: The seventies music was great: Sister Sledge, ABBA, Freda Payne – they were perfect. Then there was the classy soul stuff of George Benson, Luther Vandross and so on. And you had some great melodies from the 80s and 90s.

MARGARET HINDMAN: My dad danced in every decade from the 1940s onward. He always told me it was more important to be a good dancer than a good looker. He was always in demand as a dancer – he'd dance with women all night but always meet up with my mum for the last few tunes at the end. Even into his eighties he would dance into each corner of the hall to let other couples pass. And even if no one else was doing 'proper dancing' he said people enjoyed watching him doing it – he said it 'gladdened their hearts'. He's gone now, but he was a gentleman to the last.

DONNA WALSH: I love watching my mum and dad doing the proper ballroom stuff – they really know their moves and there's hardly ever a night that they don't end up with everyone else around them clapping them on. I missed out on that kind of dancing – to be honest I was always more of a party animal than a proper dancer. But it's brilliant that my two daughters love the TV shows and are taking real dancing lessons. With a bit of luck there'll be some young men who know the moves as well, so that when they're old enough they can enjoy what they've learned. I'm looking forward to that.

GEORGE WALLACE: Northern soul seemed to have a big revival in the 1990s and there are now well-established clubs all over the east coast and Dumfries – and we even have Glasgow coming back. All these years later you can't hear a song like the Contours' 'A Little Misunderstanding' without wanting to get up on the dance floor. Maybe you're not as fast as you used to be, but the same feeling is there after all those years.

BILL GRACIE: Nothing in life stands still. There are a couple of big bands in the Glasgow area, but what pleases me more is that some secondary schools have their own big bands now. Two schools where I live in East Kilbride have them – I've heard both and they send a tingle down my spine. I only regret that I'll probably not be around when the scene turns full circle.

ARTHUR SCOTT: The Strathpeffer Pavilion lay empty and derelict for 25 years until it was restored and reopened in 2004 to once again become a venue for concerts and dancing, among other things. In the last few years there have been a number of appearances by high profile artistes such as the Proclaimers, the Saw Doctors, Red Hot Chilli Pipers, Showaddywaddy, the Kaiser Chiefs and Deacon Blue.

It's also become a popular venue for weddings – some of those couples who met and married there in the past have now seen their children do the same thing.

I think the effect the Pavilion had on folks at the time is best summed up by a conversation I had with a long-standing acquaintance. He complained, 'Every week the Pavilion used to keep me awake until the early hours of the morning.' When I pointed out that he didn't live in Strathpeffer, he said, 'Both my daughters went to the dancin' there.' No doubt a story repeated in many households across the region!

ALAN URQUHART: We hadn't been to the dancin' in years but you never really forget the moves. When the Strictly Come Dancing programme came on, I said to my wife Ellie, 'We should start going back out.' It's easy to find wee places, even in the Highlands, where you can still have proper dances, and the internet has made it even easier.

We were a bit slow at first but it soon came back ... and of course we're going to be a bit slower because it's nearly 60 years since we first did it!

But it's our 50th wedding anniversary in 2011 and our children are putting on a family party so we've asked them to book a real dance band. They don't know it yet but we're putting together a dance routine to put the youngsters to shame. We keep laughing like youngsters ourselves when we imagine what their faces are going to be like – it's brought back great memories of when we met at the Beach Ballroom in 1957. We really are enjoying a new lease of life.

The dance goes on, as it's been going for hundreds of years. In recent times there's been resurgences of theme venues, talent shows – including karaoke – showbars and live music venues. It would be stupid to try and predict what might happen next. I've learned that. But it'll be fun finding out.

You can be sure of one thing, though: underneath the glitz and glamour, the clothes the tunes will be that age-old question that starts everything off everywhere: 'Are ye dancin?'

Index

242 SHOWBEAT
RADIO SCOTLAND'S MONTHLY
1/-
Vol. 1   No. 7   OCTOBER, 1966

STOI
EXTR

MA
TH
KN

ST
F

CROWD
ENCE PICTURE
E LATEST